How to Learn and Memorize Russian Vocabulary …

Using a Memory Palace
Specifically Designed for the
Russian Language

Anthony Metivier, PhD

Copyright © 2013 Anthony Metivier

All rights reserved.

CONTENTS

Introduction
14

Chapter One: The Main Principles
22

Chapter Two: The Main Principles
32

Chapter Three: Creating and Managing Your Russian Language Memory Palaces
43

Chapter Four: How to Extend Memory Retention Using Compounding Exercises & Generate Excitement for Learning Russian Vocabulary
69

Chapter Five: Example Memory Palace for the Letter A

74

Chapter Six: Example Memory Palace for the Letter Ж

81

Chapter Seven: Example Memory Palace for the Letter ф

84

Chapter Eight: Building Focus and Overcoming Procrastination
89

Chapter Nine: Using Relaxation to Aid the Memorization Process
95

Conclusion
98

WAIT!

I have created a Worksheet that goes along with this book. In order to receive it, send a blank email to:

learnandmemorize@zoho.com

As a reader of this book, you'll also receive a *free* subscription to the prestigious Magnetic Memory newsletter for *mysterious* memorization tips. Whilst subscriptions are currently free for readers of my books, I'm not sure how much longer I'll be making this offer. Subscribe now and get the only information that will keep your memory **_magnetic_** for years to come.

If you send an email to order the worksheets, please be sure to check your spam folder for my response and whitelist learnandmemorize@zoho.com

Why You Need To Read This Book

People around the world dream of becoming fluent in Russian, and yet so few will ever develop the vocabulary needed to express themselves in one of the world's most prominent languages. They will never use the nuances and layers of meaning unique to Russian. Even with the best intentions and the best of instructors, students of Russian struggle to learn enough words to engage in the expressive conversations needed to form important relationships, create profitable business contacts or study at schools in Russian-speaking countries.

Why is vocabulary such a struggle? Many Russian students blame a lack of time. Some claim that memorizing the words they need to know is too hard. Others try to learn by rote, desperately copying the vocabulary they want to learn hundreds of times by hand, or by playing repetitive language-learning videogames. The biggest excuse heard around the world and in every language is the saddest excuse of all: most people claim that they have a bad memory.

I sympathize with this. I used to *love* claiming that I have a poor memory. In fact, the first time I studied a foreign language, I silently swore in English so vehemently about my "bad memory" that I would have been kicked out of class had I spoken my frustration out loud.

I remained irritated with what I perceived to be my poor memory until I decided to do something about it. I studied memorization and ultimately devised the unique Memory Palace system described in this book. It is an easily learned set of skills based around the Russian alphabet that you can completely understand in under an hour. It is a system that will have you acquiring countless Russian words at an accelerated pace within just a short few hours after that. Instead of struggling to learn and retain one or two words a day, you will find yourself memorizing dozens of words every time you practice using my strategies.

Within a month of creating my own 26-letter Memory Palace system for foreign language study, I knew the meaning and sound of 260 individual and related words. Within three months, I found myself reading relatively complex fiction, poetry and newspapers, material in my target language that had previously sent me riffling through the dictionary every few seconds.

I originally developed this system to help me learn German while living in Berlin. Later, I applied the same techniques to Spanish because of the Spanish-speaking friends I made while living in Germany. In both cases, I quickly found myself conversing with people about film, music, philosophy and many other subjects that are dear to me. I was able to visit doctors and dentists without the help of a native speaker and could conduct my banking and other chores with ease. It would take this entire book to express just how many benefits I experienced, all because I took action and developed a system that enhanced my vocabulary substantially every time I practiced.

Naturally, the people around me witnessed my progress with these languages and literally interrogated me to get at my language-learning knowledge. My "guerilla" memory tactics have helped many people on their journey towards fluency, particularly because of the limited amount of time it takes to "install" my system in their minds for easy storage and retrieval of the vocabulary they have placed within their memory palaces.

It pleases me immensely to help people memorize foreign language vocabulary, especially when people regularly describe to me how easily they were able to memorize their first 100 words in under an hour using my methods. These achievements are thrilling to me, thrilling for the people who use the techniques and they will thrill you.

This edition of *How to Learn and Memorize Russian Vocabulary* is for you. Whether you are an adult, teenagers or even someone working with young children who struggle with learning, retaining and producing Russian vocabulary words. I have designed this book so that as soon as you understand the system, you can sit with a dictionary anywhere and at any time and permanently install any word that you wish for easy and accurate recall. To this end, I have written this book primarily for those Russian learners who have the burning desire to learn a word once and recall its sound and meaning without frustration of any kind within minutes, if not seconds, of having learned it.

Three obstacles stand between you and memorizing the vast quantities of Russian vocabulary you'll need to achieve your dreams of fluency.

The Belief That You Don't Need A Dedicated Memorization Strategy For Learning and Memorizing Russian Vocabulary

Although repetition is always important when it comes to any form of learning, it is a shame that so many people who study Russian wind up relying on rote learning. Audio recordings cue us to say the same phrases repeatedly with the notion that the vocabulary will remain in the mind following the automated lesson. Any of us who have tried to learn a second language has experienced the fantasy that simply repeating a phrase again and again will award us permanent ownership of those words.

I spent six months learning German in a school in Berlin. I cannot say I learned nothing because I walked away with a strong sense of German grammar and some confidence with respect to conversational speaking.

But I left the class with an extremely limited vocabulary, one based almost entirely on the cognates that German shares with English. Looking back, I'm shocked my language school at no point taught any dedicated memorization skills. Instead of sitting through long classes based upon the repetition of one or two simple discussion phrases and grammar exercises in written and oral form per class, I could have been supplementing this experience with the Memory Palace system I eventually devised for myself. With a dedicated memorization strategy, I could have been learning dozens of words per day.

The Belief That Memorization Strategies Won't Work For You

People often tell me that the memory techniques I teach will not work for them. But I always confidently respond by saying that not only will these techniques work if they as learners follow the exercises: these techniques will literally blow them away when they see how quickly their vocabulary develops.

And there is good evidence to support the use of memorization strategies in language learning. The Stanford University study conducted by Richard C. Atkinson is a representative example of many such studies that support the memorization techniques. Atkinson humorously derides the rote learning approaches taught in most foreign language classes by calling paper a "cheap memory device," one that is rather worthless compared to the memorization strategies you're about to read about and add to your palette of language learning techniques.

Atkinson concluded his study by arguing that the language-learning curriculum of all language schools and classes should include memorization techniques because students make such incredible leaps using these indisputable methods. Try out the technique taught in this book for yourself and you will marvel at the progress you'll make. Guaranteed.

The Belief That Memorization Strategies Are Too Much Work

You will need between 1-2 hours to set up the full system taught in this book and another 2-3 hours to really get the hang of the method and pick up speed. The steps are easy, fun and you can memorize new vocabulary as you are learning the system. As soon as you've understood the principles of vocabulary memorization and started working with the system taught in this book, you will be memorizing new Russian vocabulary words by the dozens with consistent speed and accuracy. The best part is that this system will serve you for life and can be extended to memorizing just about any information you could ever want.

I have a suggestion for you before you turn the page and start your journey toward advanced memorization skills. Believe in the power of your mind. When I started learning German, I constantly told myself that the language was too difficult and that my brain was ill equipped. I acted as if I had been born with a poor memory by virtue of birth.

Don't be like this. The ability to memorize large quantities of vocabulary and recall the sound and meaning of words with near-100% accuracy opened the world's doors for me, and it will do the same for you.

Moreover, when we consider the importance of Russian, it is that much more important that we do not belittle ourselves. Your mind is as powerful as mine, and by developing a positive mental attitude, learning my system and putting in a small amount of effort will be easy, fun and demonstrate to you the powerful abilities of your own mind every single day for the rest of your life.

Russian remains a language spoken all around the world. This means that those with an advanced Russian vocabulary can experience greater pleasure when traveling than they have ever dreamed possible. When it comes right down to it, isn't pleasure what life is all about?

With an advanced Russian vocabulary, you'll speak with people you might never have approached otherwise during your travels. Service will be offered to you at levels normally reserved for Russian speaking people only. If you are a businessperson, you will engage in meetings and meet potential clients and business partners with the ease and efficiency that marks all great entrepreneurs. With the system taught in this book, you will be able to enjoy Russian television, radio, newspapers and magazines much more quickly than rote learning could ever provide. You will enjoy Russian theatre and movies and even understand paintings and other art produced by Russian culture at deeper levels because you'll enjoy the ability to read the language and understand the nuances specific to those art forms.

You will love adapting this system to your individual learning style and enjoy massive success as a result. Give me 5 hours of your time as you teach yourself how to use this system and I will give you the techniques and abilities you'll need to memorize all the Russian vocabulary you have ever dreamed possible without end.

INTRODUCTION

I learned to memorize vocabulary out of desperation. Living in Berlin and spending five four-hour days a week for six months in a German language class was an amazing experience. Unfortunately, I did not learn nearly as much vocabulary as I did grammar because I did not have a deliberate strategy for memorizing the words I was learning. But I wanted one badly, and this chapter tells the story of how I came to develop the unique Memory Palace strategy taught in this book.

Before departing for Germany, I spent several weeks meeting with a small group of students in a small church in Manhattan. The teacher, while patient and clearly devoted to teaching German, had us listen to tapes of a series called *Warum Nicht?* (Why Not?) as we followed along with a textbook transcript. We then repeated the key phrases and essentially reenacted the dialogue.

I learned very little German this way. Nor in Berlin, where nearly everyone starts speaking English with you the instant they sense that your German is weak.

Although the lessons at the Hartnackschule I attended were more structured, speaking-intensive and often based on spontaneous generation of learned material, I still did not retain much vocabulary. I found this very painful because Berlin is an amazing city and the opportunity to learn German is everywhere. Unfortunately, the instant someone hears you struggling to remember particular words, they almost always begin speaking English. English has a strong presence in the country and almost everyone spoke it much better than I spoke German.

I had never been shy of rote learning, but for some reason, the hours I spent repetitively copying out the same words over and over again did little more than strain my poor wrist. Thinking I just wasn't spending enough time with the rote exercises, I actually trained myself to write with my non-dominant hand. I think this was a useful thing to do purely as a brain exercise, but it in no way helped me memorize German vocabulary.

The one word I do remember from my attempts with rote learning is *allmählich*. This is the German word for "gradually."

But I soon grew tired of learning and memorizing German vocabulary gradually. I had some familiarity with using mnemonics for my doctoral field exams and decided to look deeper into this subject. I spent countless hours online and in libraries searching for a memory system devoted specifically to language acquisition. I read countless books and listened to hours of audio programs. All of them were devoted to rote learning and I have still never found a book describing a vocabulary memorization system that lets me visualize and organize vocabulary words.

I quickly realized that I would have to create my own memorization methods. The system would have to enable me to establish new words in my mind so that I could instantly recognize them when I heard them or read them. I also wanted to be able to generate them for speaking whenever I needed them and be able to pronounce them correctly. I felt it was important for the system to reside almost entirely in my mind, though I quickly discovered that for the purposes of testing, written records would be very useful.

It never once occurred to me that designing such a technique would be easy or fun. In fact, once I found the solution, my heart was filled with dread at all the hard work it was going to be.

However, once I got started, I realized that it not only took only a short while to create the system, but it was also incredibly fun. And it made me feel good too. I believe that using the mind in this way is one of the most positive experiences a person can have.

After designing and then working with the system, it did not take me long to realize that it could be readily adapted to any language, including languages with different alphabets and sound systems.

For example, I initially found adapting the system to Russian a hard stretch. But once I worked out how to adapt my system to the Russian alphabet, I sped through Russian vocabulary acquisition with similar ease. On the way, I discovered some interesting ways to use the same Memory Palace system for remembering grammar rules, approaches that I will share with you in this book. Note, however, that this book does not purport to teach grammar in any way. Apart from sharing these few discoveries about grammar memorization, the storage and recall of vocabulary remains the main focus of this book.

Before continuing, I would like to address an issue that people constantly raise: several readers of my books and clients have told me that people who succeed with languages have a special gene that the rest of us do not. They think that this gene allows such "geniuses" to develop personalized, but still relatively formal strategies for memorizing languages.

This is nonsense. The techniques described in this book can be used by anyone.

As I noted before, many people feel that memorization techniques don't and won't work for them. This is not an attitude I accept, particularly because I used to share it. I used to love telling people about my poor memory. When we do this, we essentially train the people around us to treat us this way, which reinforces our beliefs about our inefficient memories. It is a negative cycle. I broke free by learning these skills, and the fact of the matter is that when learned and used in the correct manner, these memory techniques will change your life.

"Like a Ten-Speed bike, most of us have gears we do not use."

Charles Schultz

What I tell people who claim they have a bad

memory is that memory techniques are like bicycles. Everyone can use them. Not everybody does, but regardless of body shape, and in many cases even with certain disabilities, there are very few of us who cannot get on a bike and ride.

But bikes have adjustable parts, and like bicycles, the memory techniques taught in this book need to be adjusted by the person using them. Just as we need to re-angle the handlebars, or lower the seat on a new bike, the memory systems taught in this book will need tweaking. Once you've understood them and started to use them, you'll find ways to suit them to your brain type (as opposed to body type).

Before we continue, I'd like you to realize that learning to memorize will reward you in ways that go beyond the importance of having Russian fluency in the modern world. Using your memory to learn a new language is fun to do and, as a form of mental exercise, it sends oxygen rich blood to your brain, improving health and helping to prevent diseases like Alzheimer's and Dementia. If you don't believe me just have a glance at this interesting video:

http://www.youtube.com/watch?v=BMcduh1HEHA

But you don't have to drag yourself to the gym to achieve amazing results when it comes to working out your mind and preventing future mind illnesses. You can work out in your favorite armchair, while driving or sitting at the beach. You can develop your memory wherever you happen to be and practice the vocabulary you learn with ease because you'll have every memorized word perfectly organized within the workout gymnasium of your mind.

When it comes to learning and memorizing the vocabulary of the Russian language, there is no other book like this out there. And there is no other gymnasium quite like your mind. I do not believe in the "use it or lose it" principle, but I do know for a fact that what you do not use, you cannot benefit from. Start improving the natural abilities of your mind today.

I have written this book to train you in the basics of vocabulary acquisition, and hope that you will pass these skills on to everyone you know. It is important that you tell people about your memorization experiences because it will strengthen your personal expertise with the craft. To this end, I will show you things I tried that didn't work for me, but may work for you. And I will show you how I have adjusted some techniques that did not initially help in ways that made them more workable for me. The emphasis here is always on adjustment and adaptation. The more you work with these methods, the more you will see how you need to adapt them to your own personality and ways of thinking.

Much of this book is written in a conversational style, but each chapter ends with a set of action steps that you can use to begin implementing the techniques for yourself and think about incorporating into your classes immediately. The final chapters give you plenty of examples of how I myself work with my own Memory Palaces to learn and recall words so you can model how the system works in detail.

Finally, throughout this book, I address you not only as a learner of vocabulary memorization skills but also a potential teacher. As previously mentioned, my hope is that you will not only learn these techniques, but also pass them onto others. One of the best ways to learn a skill is to talk about what you've learned as quickly as possible. And the more people who have better memory skills, particularly when applied to language learning, the better our world becomes.

I normally don't wish my readers and students good luck on their memorization journey because my goal is to give them the tools and skills that make luck irrelevant. But you do have my warmest wishes, and I look forward to hearing the stories of your success as a result of using these methods.

Ah, but since we're here to learn and memorize Russian vocabulary, what the heck. Удачи! (This is "good luck" and is pronounced udachi or oo-duh-chee).

CHAPTER ONE: THE MAIN PRINCIPLES

There are three main principles involved in what I call "memory amplification" when teaching mnemonics to students and friends. I use this term because memory techniques do seem to "turn up the volume" of the mind. Many learners respond positively to this concept because it is easy to imagine their minds as radios "tuning in" on a signal and having a volume knob they can turn up in order to increase the receptivity of their minds.

After we learn these principles, I'm going to show you have to use them to memorize the Russian alphabet first and then how to memorize Russian vocabulary.

The three principles you will learn in this chapter: **location, imagery**, and **activity**. Along with these principles, we will talk about **Preparation** and **Predetermination.**

These are ancient principles that have been used for thousands of years. However, it is only recently that I have elaborated them into a dedicated system for memorizing vocabulary.

Nonetheless, if you are interested in the history of memory techniques, I highly recommend reading this webpage:

http://www.mundi.net/cartography/Palace.

Joshua Foer's recent book *Moonwalking with Einstein: The Art and Science of Memory* is also fantastic, but please be advised that this book covers more cultural history than specific guidance when it comes to building memory palaces for language acquisition. But if you're serious about finding classroom methodologies that will directly impact how you absorb, retain and recall Russian vocabulary, then you have everything to gain by reading all that you can on the topic of memorization, including Foer's book.

Let's now look at each of the three main principles in turn. Keep in mind that each of principles is individually important and each is interrelated with the other. Use them independently, and they will still help improve your memory. Use them together and your memory skills will soar beyond belief.

Location

Location is part of, but not the entire picture of the memory palace concept. Locations are the Memory Palaces we will use to store imagery. They are based on real places that we are familiar with from our every day lives.

The reason we use locations to memorize Russian vocabulary is because we tend to remember places we've been without exerting any effort, and this is one of the key principles of memory work: eliminate everything that you don't have to work at remembering and build natural associations in those familiar places.

When thinking about locations for storing memories, try doing something that I did for myself. I once determined that I have lived in eight cities, twenty-five houses (or apartments) and sixteen neighborhoods within those cities. I have yet to count all the familiar houses that belong to my friends and extended family members, but surely the number is exponential.

Plus, the availability of locations is expanding all the time as I continue to meet new people and visit new places. There are even hotel rooms that I remember very well during stays all over the world. Then there is the path I took from a hotel in Paris to the Louvre. The short journey made such an impact on me that it has served me very well over the years. The point is that we all have more territory in our minds than we could ever possibly hope to use for storing memories. The best part is that we can then sub-divide locations into individual stations. When you consider each apartment, home or building a "location," then each individual room will be a station within that location.

Going through your mind and identifying the countless locations and all the individual stations you are familiar with is not difficult work. It is tremendously pleasurable and will amaze you when you consciously begin to realize just how much geography you hold in your mind.

As I'm going to discuss further on, I like to combine indoors and outdoors locations, all places that I know very well. There are some advanced ways that I use imaginary locations as well, and I will teach you these in one of the bonus chapters that accompanies this book.

I think that as a teacher, you'll be impressed by the power of location in storing memories and probably see how you can use imaginary locations as well. However, for memorizing Russian vocabulary effectively, I suggest that you always use locations that you are familiar with.

How can you judge familiarity? It's quite simple. If you can wander through a location in your mind without pausing to think about what room comes next, you can effectively work with this "palace." The notion of moving from room to room works especially well because the order of rooms within a familiar building is difficult to forget.

Outside locations, on the other hand, can be difficult to remember. In such cases, it is better to use landmarks. Landmarks could include the entrance to your house, the driveway, the yards of the houses on your street and the merry-go-round and swing set in a local park.

You could also use streets in a neighborhood, assuming that you remember them with ease and without having to search your mind for them. If you live in a town with numbered streets and avenues, these can be especially useful because a progression of numbers up or down is concrete. But if you are moving through a park where one tree looks much like the next, you will likely find yourself struggling as you move through your palace.

It cannot be said often enough: the more you use places you already know, the less you have to remember. The less you have to remember, the more you can associate the sounds of the words with their meanings in memorable ways. And the more you can associate, the more you can remember. It's an awkward equation, I know, but it all boils down to the fact that remembering less leads to remembering more.

Imagery

Imagery is ... well, imagery: mental pictures that you build in your mind. For the purposes of memorization, these pictures need to be big and colorful. The larger and the more colorful, the better. You want to exaggerate the size and colors because the larger and more colorful the image, the more memorable it will be. This will in turn strengthen the associations.

Some of the students I've taught tell me that they are not particularly visual in their imaginations and I completely understand this. In fact, when I read a novel, I rarely see images in my mind. Reading is almost always a conceptual experience for me. In fact, it's possible that I have something called *Imagination Deficit Disorder* or IDD.

Whether I suffer this condition or not, I do have a low visual threshold in my mind, so am able to give my non-visual students a few suggestions based on my own experiences.

First, if a student can't think in color, tell them not to force it. Have them try thinking in black and white, taking care to exaggerate both the black and white. Exactly how black is the black and how white is the white? Is there an opportunity to use gray in some memorable way?

Whatever happens, we should never allow a lack of imagination for intense imagery to be a barrier.

In the event that neither color nor black and white patterns prove useful to you, try associating certain prefixes with actors or fictional characters. For instance, let's say you are trying to memorize words that start with "inter" (interact, intercept, interstate). Every word that begins with "inter" can be automatically associated with, say, Anne Hathaway, who played an intern in *The Devil Wears Prada*. I realize that not a great number of words that begin with "inter," but isolating parts of words is a key principle of effectively using memory palaces to store and retrieve vocabulary until the "training wheels" on the bike of memory, i.e. the mnemonics, can fall away.

Another option for non-visual learners is to use paintings. Choose and study paintings that you are familiar with for your memory palace imagery. The more you are aware of the intricacies of famous paintings, the better.

The next time you are in an art gallery or looking through an art book, pay closer attention to what you are looking at. Buy books about art history and specific painters and scrounge through them for ideas. Spend time imagining what zany actions these famous figures could be engaged in. The ideas generated in such exercises could become fodder for better associations while memorizing Russian vocabulary as you involve the associations with movement. We'll talk more about adding action to your images momentarily.

Another idea, perhaps one for advanced memorizers, is to select a number of famous paintings and place these in a memorable order inside of an imaginary art gallery. As you mentally walk from painting to painting in the art gallery of your mind, you can place your associations in front of each painting. For instance, the word "interim" could have Anne Hathaway engaged in Internet marketing (generating the *im* in interim) in front of a painting with an imp.

The drawback to this method is that it requires memorizing the order of several paintings with which to make word associations. Nonetheless, I provide it as an idea for conceptual learners and for those who might respond to this approach.

I must mention a small problem with artwork, however. Paintings and statues tend to be static. They don't move. That said, if you can imagine the Mona Lisa walking like an Egyptian outside of her frame, or Michelangelo's David doing the Moonwalk, then you should have no problem.

Finally, you can use toys that you remember. GI Joe, Barbie, My Little Pony, Hello Kitty! ... anything goes. As with paintings, however, the most important factor here is that you can put these figures into action. Without action, the memories most likely will not stick in your mind nearly as well.

So without further adieu, let's turn our attention to the matter of ...

Action

By now, you will have thought about for yourself different locations you are familiar with, sub-locations or stations within those locations and different ways that you can use exaggerated imagery to boost the stickiness of the words lodged in your various stations.

The next step is to give your images a bit of movement.

More than a bit, actually. Just as you want to exaggerate the size and color of your images, you also want to exaggerate their actions.

It's not an entirely nice way to think of memorization, but something that will work wonders for you is to make the action violent. Highway accidents serve as an example of how memorable scenes of violence can be – even in their aftermath. If after seeing an accident or accident site you could not shake the memory of your mind, then you know how powerful violent images can be.

This is not to suggest that lives need to be lost when working in your memory palaces. Cartoon violence will work just as well. Wile E. Coyote, for instance, provides a strong example of someone willing to savage himself in some pretty hilarious ways when trying to make the Road Runner his dinner.

Again, the object is to create something so potently memorable that working hard to recall the image is unnecessary. It will instantly come to mind when you look for it because you've given yourself no other choice. You've made the image impossible to forget.

Now, you may be thinking that using this technique is going to lead to a brain cluttered with bizarre images, especially since you already have enough new information to deal with in terms of memorizing the sounds and meanings of your new words.

Your may experience such clutter in the beginning when first learning the techniques. With practice, however, you will learn to be clear and precise.

Moreover, the images used in the associations tend to eventually fall away, leaving the actual memory intact. You'll still wander your palaces and have a hankering of what the images you once used to memorize a word, but these fragments will be secondary.

For example, I initially associated the German word "zerbrechlich" (breakable) with a vase being smashing by Zorro on an escalator in the Sony Centre movie theatre in Berlin. But although I remember the word and what it means perfectly well, I never actually have to visit that place in my mind anymore, nor do I have to imagine Zorro breaking the vase. I can if I want to, but because I spent time making sure the image was strong enough in the beginning and did the compounding exercises I discuss in a future chapter, the image very quickly loses importance as fluency takes over.

In sum, the new word and its meaning will be the central artifact on display in your mind. If the entire memorization system is indeed like a bicycle, then the images themselves are the training wheels. They are not necessarily meant to stay after you've grown with the system. The images are the tools we use to install the images, and although we will remember what they were, so long as we continue using the word by reading, speaking and writing, we reduce the chances that we will need the tools.

If you do not like the bicycle metaphor (i.e. the idea that you need to "adjust" each of these principles to your own way of learning the way you would raise or lower the seat on a new bike, etc.), another way to think about this is in terms of dental implants.

When dentists create an implant for a patient, they not only have to order a specifically shaped screw to drill into the bone, but they have to order a ratchet designed specifically for turning that custom-made screw. Sure, the dentist keeps the tool in case the implant needs to be retracted, but as a dental practitioner, the goal is to do such a good job that the tool will no longer be necessary. But it will be there if needed.

Let's now move on to the next two principles.

Preparation and Predetermination

Like the full memory palace organization system revealed in an upcoming chapter, Preparation and Predetermination are two memory skills that I have not seen talked about in any other memory books, apart from those I have written for memorizing other languages. Yet, both of these steps are essential elements to memorization success when using memory palaces to tackle vocabulary, or for that matter, anything you might like to remember.

Preparation, to begin, involves relaxing the mind. I will share several thoughts about how best to relax in the concluding chapter, but for now, please realize that when the mind is tense, busy or exhausted, it will resist attempts at memorization.

This fact does not mean that you won't be able to remember anything. It only means that their minds will not be in the most receptive state possible. But when your mind is open and relaxed, you'll be amazed by how these techniques will double, triple and even quadruple their results. Even a three-minute meditation before memorizing can work miracles, but see the conclusion for a larger list of possibilities.

Predetermination, on the other hand, involves charting out the memory locations and stations *before* attempting to place the words to be memorized in the memory palace system. I must stress that before you populate your memory palaces with Russian vocabulary, you should consider building the entire system first – or at least a substantial portion of it. I've tried making up my palaces as I went along, and I can tell you that this leads to little more than frustration and impoverished results. So please spend the necessary time to predetermine the locations and label the individual stations within them.

Before continuing, I want to stress that perfection is not the goal with either of these two principles. Preparation and predetermination work best when not forced, so it's important not to harm our forward movement by being too particular about every little detail. We just want to get the basic layout in place so that we can work relatively quickly with the words we want to memorize.

Preparing Your First Location

It helps a great deal to draw maps of the locations you will be using and have some system for labeling the individual stations. Alternatively, students can list them in a Word document or catalog them in an Excel file. You can also easily send a blank email to learnandmemorize@zoho.com and I will send you free Magnetic Memory Worksheets that will allow you to simply fill in the details.

Take advantage of this offer right now because these worksheets will help you instantly organize your locations and the stations within them. All you have to do is fill in the blanks. You'll also get a free subscription to the Magnetic Memory mailing list, which gives you access to helpful tips about amplifying your memory, inspirational notes, links to valuable videos and other memorization-related materials that will keep your mind magnetic for years to come.

Some students I've had like to sketch the different rooms or use computer architectural programs to create digital layouts. Although I personally don't go that far, I tend to do all three of the former in order to maximize the strength of the associations I'll be making.

Let's face it: If we're going to spend time learning a language, we want the vocabulary to stay in our heads. Learning grammar is pointless if you haven't got plenty of words to fit into the equations. It's worth taking the time to fully realize my palaces so that they will be accessible when I need them for near-instantaneous recall when reading and conversing.

The first Memory Palace I ever created was my apartment in Schöneberg-Berlin. It had 8 stations, though I now recommend and always make sure that any new memory palace I've started has at least 10.

This particular apartment was on the Feurigstraße, which means "fiery street." The name came from the fact that a fire station was located just a few blocks north of me. This was rarely a bother because the firemen had the lovely habit of only turning the sirens on after they had left the street.

I don't mention this to be cute or self-indulgent. All of these details come in very handy when it comes to building Memory Palaces.

First, because the apartment was on Feurigstraße, I used that apartment and every station in that palace to remember words that begin with the letter 'F.' I could use this apartment for any other letter, but this is the association that came to me naturally, and I think it is best to allow for such natural associations.

Because I don't have to spend any time remembering that all 'F' words are connected with the Feurigstraße palace, I don't have to make any odd leaps in my mind searching for words that start with "F." Had I placed 'S' words there, then it would take my mind a step to search for which palace has 'S' in it.

Don't worry. I'm going to go into greater detail about all of this later. But for now, the basic principle is that every location is a Memory Palace and as much as possible, that location should start with the same letter of the words that you will store there.

The Feurigstraße apartment had a nice layout:

1. My Office
2. Laundry Room
3. Bathroom
4. Bedroom
5. Wife's office
6. Living Room
7. Hallway
8. Kitchen

Later, I extended this palace outside of the apartment:

9. Outside of the door
10. Stairwell
11. Front door
12. Parking garage
13. Sidewalk
14. Used book store
15. Playground
16. Fire station
17. Church
18. Sushi restaurant

… and so forth

There are two important points that I need to mention here. In creating these "journeys" through the stations of a Memory Palace, you need to structure your progress in such a way that you:

a) Never cross your own path

b) Never trap yourself

If, when you are rehearsing or searching for your words, you have to cross your own path, you are liable to confuse yourself. You will find yourself pausing to remember how exactly the journey went, and such interruptions will impede your recall. Therefore, it is best to create a journey that follows a straight line. Even with great experience in the art of memorization, this principle will remain key.

Second, it is important that you don't trap yourself. The reason I was able to add more stations to my 'F' Memory Palace so easily after I finished with my initial 8 is because I started at a terminal point in the apartment: my office. Had I started in the kitchen and moved toward my office, I would have trapped myself – unless I wanted to jump off the small balcony and down onto the street, that is.

Making an imaginative leap from the balcony to the street is entirely possible, but it is unnatural, and nothing I would do in reality. Thus, such an action causes the mind unnecessary work. The point of this memorization strategy is to *always* reduce the amount of work your mind has to do in order to get to the associations that will prompt the sound and meaning of the words you want to recall.

Therefore, although you will be exaggerating shapes, colors and actions in your memory work, I feel that it is best to keep the path you take through the palaces as natural and free from exaggeration as possible. Save anything that requires your memory for the things you want to remember and eliminate all else.

In each of those stations in a Memory Palace, I would then place individual words and use the principles of imagination and action to make them memorable.

Here is an equation that you might find useful:

Location/station = Word

Image = pronunciation

Action = meaning

We're going to go into that equation in greater detail soon, but for now, it is important to understand the basic organizational layout of a Memory Palace and spend a bit of time constructing one by obeying the principles laid out in this chapter.

Try this method out for yourself. Describe the layout of the place you live in now and make a list of at least 10 individual stations. You can make a handmade list or use an Excel file. There is good reason to get started with Excel files right away for the purposes of testing the strength of your memorizations in the future.

Before we close this chapter with a list of steps you can take to get started immediately, here are some final tips about creating memorable imagery:

1. **Clarity:** Make sure that the images you create are

clear. I always talk about exaggerating your images, making them colorful, vibrant and as large as possible, but they should also stand out clearly in your mind. I've decreased the amount of time I need to spend substantially by focusing on the clarity of my images, and also by focusing on how they stand in relation to the Memory Palace. It seems that the more clear my Memory Palaces and the more clear my associative imagery, the more the two Magnetically fuse together.

2. **Precision of detail**: It takes only a second to focus on the details. If you are using a chicken to memorize something, what kind of chicken is it? A fat chicken, skinny chicken, red chicken, white chicken, chicken-in-boots with a cigarette hanging out of its beak - and if so, what kind of cigarette? Can the brand of the cigarette help trigger the target material you are memorizing? There is tremendous Magnetic wealth in the details.

3. **Avoid relevance:** A lot of people I talk to and discuss the Magnetic Memory system with often try to make their associative imagery relevant. Granted, one should seize on coincidences. They happen all the time during my memorization sessions and work gangbusters for me. Normally, however, it is much better when the images are absurd and have seemingly nothing to do with the target material whatsoever. You could call this the principle of

contrast, which is to say that the more the image sticks out like a sore thumb in your exquisitely magnetized Memory Palace, the easier it will come to mind when you call for it.

4. **Avoid logic:** This point is almost the same, but differs in the fact that many people who describe their efforts to me put too much logic into the narrative elements of their image associations. They make pretty little vignettes that make sense. I'm sorry, dear Memorizer of Russian vocabulary, but things that make sense are not always sensible. Certainly not when it comes to memorization.

Here's an example I heard from a coaching client once upon a time: "The Statue of Liberty is leaning down to pick up her torch when Godzilla kicks her in the rump." This is a memorable image, I have to admit, but why is she picking up her torch? That's logical. It sucks the memorability out of the image. Why not have her picking up Salvador Dali's mustaches or a giant pig with Mount Rushmore tattooed on its flank? Having her pick up her torch is *congruent* with reality. Having her pick up a piano made of sandwiches lacks congruency, and is thereby far more memorable.

Keep these four tips in mind as you create your images and you will be very successful with your memorization of Russian vocabulary.

Here are some actions steps that will help you master the techniques taught in this chapter and give you ideas for how to help your friends and families learn the techniques too. Obviously, you should not be teaching something that you yourself haven't had success with.

1. Select at least 10 different locations that you remember well. If you are feeling motivated, you can list all 33 giving you locations enough for the entire alphabet. These locations could be apartments or houses you've lived in, schools, libraries, workplaces or art galleries. All that matters is that you know them well and can walk around them in your mind. I find that movie theatres with multiple screening rooms work really well for me, and as a film professor, I have over a dozen theatres that I am intimately familiar with.

2. Select and list at least 10 "stations" within each of the locations you've listed. These different stations will become the places you will leave each of the words you want to memorize within each palace. These stations can be entire rooms, which I recommend when you are just getting started, or they can be more specific. You could use an armchair and then the lamp table beside it as two different stations, for instance. Even though you will not need to remember any of these individual stations (that's the whole point), you should still

write them down for the purpose of testing the strength and rigor of your memorizations.

3. Take a walk through each palace and the stations that you have identified. While wandering, make each and every station vivid in your mind. You can imagine cleaning everything out if you like, removing all the dust and dirt that can get in the way of your memorization process.

4. Draw maps. Creating visual representations of each location and the stations within them can be very powerful and save you a lot of testing time later. You definitely don't want to be vague about what comes next in your Memory Palaces. Again, using an Excel file is also a great idea if you are not a visual person, though doing both is highly recommended.

5. Practice remembering trivial things where there is no pressure if you make mistakes. The top ten highest mountains or largest rivers make for great practice. Shopping lists also make for good practice. Remember to make everything large and colorful.

6. Include action. Let's say you're trying to remember that you need carrots on your shopping list. Imagine that you are jumping on the carrot and hurting it badly. You can use whatever image comes to your mind, so

long as it is over-the-top, hilarious, zany and memorable. If you relax, you'll find that your mind will come up with material very naturally.

7. On that point, always practice in a state of relaxation. I have included specific notes on the best relaxation techniques for memorization in the final chapter. These relaxation practices are also good for any form of creativity.

8. Make sure that you are having fun. If not, take a break and come back to it. When you start out practicing with memory items that have no consequence, you enable yourself to play freely with the concept. If, for example, you start with Russian vocabulary right away, you risk associating frustration with the language you've always dreamed of learning. Make sure that you can memorize at least ten items you know nothing about before attempting any words. For example, you could memorize the ten tallest mountains in order of size. Or you could work on one of the bonus exercises included at the end of this book.

9. Give yourself an exam. As I've stressed, you need to write everything down for the purposes of testing. This is not rote learning. It's a method of giving you the ability to double check. Also, when testing, don't look at the original list you created. Write out everything fresh and then

compare the list you wrote out from memory with the original. I've created this video for you to refer to when it comes to testing your memorization work: How to Use Excel Files to Support Your Memory Palaces.

http://www.youtube.com/watch?v=UMPMuOyfke4

10. Teach. The best way to truly learn a technique is to teach it to someone else. You should discuss your newfound knowledge about memorization as often as possible because this will deepen your familiarity with the techniques and prove to yourself and others that these things really do work. It's not showing off to do so. You'll also be making the world a better place because you'll be enabling others to use their minds more effectively. Make working on your own memory and helping others improve theirs. This should be a habit for life.

CHAPTER TWO:
APPLYING THE MAIN PRINCIPLES TO LEARNING AND MEMORIZING THE RUSSIAN ALPHABET & RUSSIAN VOCABULARY

This chapter explains the complete system for creating and using a 33-letter Memory Palace system for Russian. By this time, you've already created at least 10 locations for yourself based on places you remember with ease, and ideally, fondness. You've made sure that all of the material is charted them out either on paper or using an Excel file for testing purposes and that these list at least 10 stations within the 10 locations.

Memorizing the Alphabet

In order to memorize the Russian alphabet, we first need to create a Memory Palace that has 33 stations. Although there are some non-vocalized letters, I recommend that you memorize these along with all the others so that you know what they are when you see them.

33 stations in a Memory Palace may seem like a lot, so I invite you to email me at for a subscription to the Magnetic Memory newsletter. You will find literally dozens of ideas to help you build your Memory Palaces effectively if you struggle with the ideas presented in this book. I answer questions from readers and frequently offer special promotions and free gifts that enable people to memorize foreign vocabulary in ways that are easy, fast and fun.

In order to remember the sound of each letter, we need to create both a visual picture of the letter and an action that helps "trigger" the sound so that we can orally reproduced it.

The best way to explain this further is to simply invite you to take a tour into my Memory Palace where I store the Russian Alphabet.

I use the high school where I attended Grade 10. It was very easy to find 33 stations for this Memory Palace by following the Magnetic Memory principles laid out in this book.

To briefly repeat them: I start at a terminal location

that ensures I will never be trapped and carefully construct my journey so that I do not cross my own path.

Although Memory Palaces used to store alphabets are what I call "limited set" Memory Palaces (which is to say that they do not need to be extended to include more stations), I still try to obey the principle of being able to add on new stations if I want to. For example, in the case of Russian, I might want to memorize some of the letters that used to be in the Russian alphabet, but were later removed.

Although that's perhaps trivia for people fascinated with language in general, there's another reason to make sure your Memory Palaces are open-ended. By having more places to add, you avoid "Memory Palace Claustrophobia," which is a merely psychological problem some of my coaching clients have had. It's the feeling that there isn't enough space for the images they have created. I've even had some people who use more than one station to memorize a single letter in the beginning, and for reasons like this, it is always very useful to add one more station.

Let's begin. Although I don't expect you to follow along on my journey as if it were your own, I want you to get a sense of how you can do this for yourself by charting out 33 separate stations in a

Memory Palace. Before starting on your own Memory Palace, it's important to do what I have done: walk through an area you are intimately familiar with it and see it as vividly in your mind as you can. Then go back through it and identify 33 different stations and chart these out using a top-down list, an Excel file, or a map that you've drawn for yourself. You will use these for the purposes of testing your memorizations based on the image-action associations you'll be building for yourself.

For the purposes of this example Memory Palace for the Russian alphabet, I'm going to show you the stations by name and number, the Russian letter and the image/action I used to memorize how it sounds. If you would like to hear how the alphabet sounds and have a graphic representation of it before your eyes as you listen, please visit:

http://en.wikipedia.org/wiki/Russian_alphabet

You might also want to read/listen to *How to Pronounce Russian Correctly* by Tania Bobrinskoy and Irina Gsovskaya. (Passport Books, 1991).

In fact, it is important for you to listen to a native speaker pronounce the alphabet because some of the ways I will describe the sound will help, but not necessarily play out the same way in the ears of your mind as they do in mine. As with many parts of the Magnetic Memory system, your participation is required, and a great exercise is to listen to a native speaker pronounce the letter and then write out an English representation of the letter as you hear it in your mind. For example, I would represent the sound of **Г** as *gay-ah*, but it might sound more like *gay-eh* to you. Thus, it is essential that you adapt these *homophonic transliterations* to your own style (more on the art and science of homophonic transliteration to come).

One: Outside of front door: **A**. To remember that A in Russian is pronounced "ah," I see my doctor forcing one of those wooden sticks in my mouth and telling me to say "ah." Following the Magnetic Memory principles, I make the image large, bright, colorful and filled with action. It's not just that I have the wooden stick in my mouth, I see him forcing it into my mouth. This makes the image doubly memorable.

Two: Inside of front door: **Б**. This letter is pronounced something like "b-ay" when recited on its own in the context of the Russian alphabet, but will usually sound something like the "b" in "box." To remember the sound of **Б** as an indepentend letter and remember that it is normally sounded as it would in English for *box*, I see a horde of angry movie fans stuffing film director and producer Michael **Bay** into a box to prevent him from making another terrible *Transformers* film.

Three: Heather's locker (I'm traveling to the right in my Memory Palace version of this high school): **В**. This is pronounced like something between "veh" and "vyeh." It's the kind of "v" sound we would use in English to pronounce "voice." I see guitarist David Mustaine riding his flying-v guitar the way a witch rides a broom as my friend Heather tries to catch him (she had the hots for him back when we were young – and maybe she still does).

Four: Janitor's office door: **Г**. This is the Russian equivalent of our "g," but it is pronounced "gay" with a slight "ah" sound at the end, i.e. "gay-ah." Since **Г** looks like a walking stick, I see the janitor rushing out of his office trying to beat me with it while accusing me of being "gay-ah." (Note: I do not consider this a slur. Memorization techniques often involve being politically incorrect and sometimes associating the target material one wants to learn with unpleasant images and themes).

Five: David's locker. **Д**. This is the equivalent of "d" in English. It has a slight "d-ay" sound to it. For whatever reason, this letter reminds me of a crab scuttling along with one black eye. I hear him shouting "seize the day!" but also see this in an exaggerated cartoon speech balloon spelled Дау.

Six: Front of Gym Entrance Door #1. **Е**. It can be frustrating to see a letter like this and yet have to pronounce it something like "yeah." To help myself out, I see a giant letter "E" dressed in a basketball jersey with "yeah" printed it on it and jumping up and down while shouting the same.

Seven: Directly Inside the Gym Entrance Door #1: **Ё**. This letter sounds like "yo." Here I again use the E with the jersey. This time, however, he is pounding at two dots over his head with a badminton racket will shouting "yo!" (His jersey now says "yo" as well to help compound the power of the memorization – more on "compounding in a future chapter).

Eight: East side basket ball net. **Ж**. This is the equivalent of our "j," but it sounds more like "j-eh" or perhaps "zhe." You can think of it like the way the "s" sounds in the English word "pleasure." In this image, I see a giant June bug playing basketball – using another June bug as the ball. The ball is shouting "jeh/zhe no!"

Nine: North Wall bleachers, East side. **З**. This letter is pronounced "zeh" or "ze" and is often like the "z" in "zoo" when used in combination with other letters. Here I see a snake curled into a backwards three hissing "ze ze ze" at a box of McDonald's French fries. The McDonald's logo, in this case rearranged as a **З** helps reinforce the shape of **З** and its association with the snake making the sound of this letter as it hisses.

Ten: West side basketball net. **И**. This letter sounds like "ee" as in "meat." I see a backwards n, i.e. **И** playing basketball with a ball made of of steak, i.e. meat.

Eleven: Equipment locker. **Й**. This letter is pronounced quite differently than it is used in most words. It is usually used like the "y" in boy, or the "y" in yoga, but to say the letter out loud sounds something like "ee-krat-kai-ye" (again, be sure to hear a native speaker pronounce it and create a version of your own in English as you would write it. This is the principle of homophonic transliteration that we will be going over in greater detail later). To remember **Й**, I see a eagle (ee) with a crab in his beak (cra) who has a kite in its claw (kai) that has the word "yellow" on it (ye).

Twelve: Inside of Gym Entrance door #2: **К**. This is the equivalent of our "k," but pronounced "ka," as in "kite" or "cat." Here I see a giant *ca*t trying to eat a giant **К**.

Thirteen: Outside of Gym Entrance door #2: **Л**. This is the English equivalent of "l," or "el," as used in words like "lamp" and "light." The letter looks like a thin "j" stood next to a bolded "I," so I see those two letters together as Lex Luthor (his name compounds the association to the sound of "l") pounds at them with his bald head.

Fourteen: Dino's locker: **M**. This letter doesn't need a whole lot of razzmatazz imagery, so I just see Dino painting the letter M in red with Peter Lorre – who starred in Fritz Lang's masterpiece film *M* – shouts in terror for his **momm**y. Again – these exaggerations may seem excesses, but they are absolutely essential to information retention when using the Magnetic Memory method.

Fifteen: Mr. Sheeley's classroom door. **H**.

Before I continue, I want to make a note about using classrooms and rooms in general.

One of the principles of the Magnetic Memory system is that we don't cross our own path. A lot of people have asked me over the years, how can one enter a room and then leave it without crossing one's own path.

There are two answers:

First, this may be one instance where you can break that rule. You'll just need to experiment.

Second, I think it's best to simply stand in your imagination at the door and peer into the room without actually walking through it. You still create a continuous mini-journey in the room, but you don't actually walk into it. For more tips and tricks that will expand your knowledge of how to avoid common errors and confusion, send an email right now to learnandmemorize@zoho.com.

Now back to our regularly scheduled alphabet.

In Russian, **H** sounds like our "n." In order to memorize this, I see an "H" kissing an "N" while making a "nnnnnnn" sound to express pleasure.

Sixteen: Sheeley's Back black board: **O**. To my ear, it sounds like native speaker's pronounce this "oh-ah," but you'll have to hear it for yourself. In this case, I see a monkey drawing a giant **O** while shouting "oh-ah!.

Seventeen: Sheeley's classroom window, right side: **П**. This letter is equivalent to our "p," and sounds in words as we would say "pet," but alone sounds something like "pay." To memorize this, I see Mr. Sheeley **pay**ing money into a bank machine shaped like **П**.

Eighteen: Sheeley's classroom window, left side: **P**. This letter is like our "r" (as in "rock"), but is pronounced "er" as in "heir." To remember this, I see Mr. Sheeley breaking the diagonal leg off of an "R." This "R" (now a "P") has a big mouth that is saying, " errrr, excuse me ..."

Nineteen: Mr. Sheeley's desk: **C**. In Russian, **C** is pronounced like our "s," for use in words like "sun." To remember this, I see a crescent moon, (i.e. a "C") on Mr. Sheeley's desk taking a bite out of the sun.

Twenty: Mr. Sheeley's world map: **Т**. This is the equivalent of our "t," but pronounced "tay." I see a tiger swiping at Mr. Sheeley's map with an old cassette **ta**pe of K.C. and the Sunshine Band's "Shake Your Boot-tay."

Twenty-one: Dave's locker: **У**. This is pronounced "oo" as in "soon." I see Dave with a giant **У** hammer pounding a l**oo**n into his locker.

Twenty-two: Stair-case door: **Ф**. This is "ef," not unlike how our "f" would be used in the word "food." This letter reminds me very much of an Olympic torch, so I see one lighting the door on fire.

Twenty-three: First ten stairs: **Х**. This letter is pronounced something like "chk-hay," (the "k" is very subtle). It's kind of like the "ch" in words like "loch" when pronounced by a Scotsman, as in "the Loch Ness monster." To remember this, I see two Loch Ness monsters fighting each other in the form of an **Х**. As ever, the image is large, bright, vivid and filled with action.

Twenty-four: Stair-case landing: **Ц**. This letters sounds like "tse," sort of like the "ts" in "boo**ts**." Here I see mechanic bolting a tiny tail onto a large letter "u." But instead of using normal mechanical equipment, he is using a large pair of boots to perform the operation.

Twenty-five: Next ten stairs: **Ч**. This letter sounds like "ch-eh" and is used in words in a way that sounds like how we would use "ch" in words like "chat." To memorize this, I see this funny "Y" shape balancing the letters "c" and "h" on its arms while Che Guevara swats at them with a machine gun.

Twenty-six: Top landing: **Ш**. This letter has a "sha" sound, and would be used as we use "sh" in words like "sheet." I see this letter actually spreading out bed sheets on the top landing of the staircase and jumping up and down singing: "sha na na na, sha na na na …"

Twenty-seven: Top stairs door: **Щ**. This letter is very similar to the previous, but it sounds longer, more like "sh-cha." It's definitely important to hear this one spoken by a native. To memorize **Щ**, I see the mechanic again. This time he's bolting a tail onto the previous letter using a piece of fre**sh** **ch**eese. That image helps reinforce the long "sh-cha" sound.

Twenty-eight: My locker: **Ъ**. This letter is pronounced something like "tah-vio-rdee-zeh-nack." It's actually not sounded as such, but changes the sounds of the letters it is placed beside, typically to make them harder. I see a little "b" with a hat, (i.e. **ъ**) carrying a TV and declaring "I want a snack."

Twenty-nine: Biology classroom door: **Ы**. This letter sounds somewhere between "b-we" and "v-we." It can also sound like how our "i" sounds like in words like "skill." To memorize it, I see that same elf with a giant staff banging on the side of the door as he peers in. He is saying "bweve-iology" to remind me of the sound of this letter.

Thirty: Side storage cabinet: **ь**. This letter has no sound, but often softens the letter it is found beside. To pronounce it by name, the word sounds something like "mya-gkiz-zna-ck." To memorize this I have a cat meowing over a Petri dish filled with keys. The cat is begging for a snack.

Thirty-one: Bunsen burner station: **Э**. This letter sounds like something between "eh-ya" and "eh-er." It reminds me a lot of the Euro currency symbol, so I see some students burning Euro using the Bunsen burners. The teacher is running to stop them, shouting: "hey, yeah!" That doesn't necessarily make sense, but it doesn't have to. It just needs to be memorable.

Thirty-two. Back desk I used to sit at: **Ю**. This letter is pronounced something like "yo," with a slightly extended "oh" sound at the end. It is often used like the "u" in the English word "use." Looked at from above, the device used to hold a beaker over the flames of a Bunsen burner looks a lot like **Ю**. So I see myself looking down at that while lighting a Bunsen burner. But the device jumps up and brands the symbol onto my forehead for life. "Yo!" I shout in agony.

Thirty-three: Front chalk board: **Я**. This letters sounds like "ya," the way Germans say "yes" (i.e. "ja"). In Russian words, it often sounds like the "y" sound in words like "yardstick." To memorize this, I see myself drawing a backwards "R" with a giant yardstick.

Memorizing the Alphabet Conclusion

Now that you've seen how I created my Memory Palace journey for memorizing the sounds and shapes of the Russian alphabet, you should be able to do the same.

This process took me approximately 45 minutes from start to finish. Once you're done, you should be able to mentally walk through the entire alphabet and correctly pronounce each letter, both forwards and backwards. In fact, moving forwards and backwards is not only great proof of how powerful the use of Memory Palaces can be, but is also great exercise for the brain.

Creating Your Memory Palaces for Each Letter of the Alphabet

The next step, once you are familiar with the alphabet, is to create a new, individual Memory Palace for each and every letter (I recommend you create Memory Palaces for the unsounded letters as well for the purposes of completion).

Here's how I work whenever setting myself up to memorize the essential vocabulary I will need to operate in a new language.

First, I create a folder and then create multiple Excel files. Excel works the best because it eliminates the need to build a table. However, you can just as easily build a table using Microsoft Word, Pages or whatever Word Processing software you happen to be using.

In this case, the files or individual sheets of paper for each palace need to create correspond to the 33 letters of the Russian alphabet. In the following example, I will show you what my selected locations for Russian vocabulary will be. Naturally, I used a completely different set of locations when I was working on German.

А = Alan's House

Б = Brock Video Store

How to Learn and Memorize Russian Vocabulary

В = Valleyview Liquor Store

Г = Gary's House

Д = Dawn's House

Е = Eric's House

Ё = York University Ross Building

Ж = Janet's House

З = Zoltan's Movie House

И = Toronto Eaton Center

Й = Lee's House

К = Katrin's House

Л = Lyle's Apartment

М = Mom's House

Н = Nola's Apartment

О = Owen's House

П = Paul's House

Р = Rick's house

С = Samantha's House

Т = Trevor's House

У = Uncle Lloyd's House

Ф = Frank's Apartment

Х = Kane's House

Ц = Tristan's House

Ч = Che's House (Not that Che! This refers to a writer friend of mine who lives in Pittsburgh).

Ш = Shane's House

Щ = Doctor's office (where the secretary's name is Sheila)

Ъ = Tammy's House

Ы = Brandy's House

Ь = Manny's House

Э = Evan's House

Ю = Jan's Apartment

Я = My Apartment (**Я** is the Russian word for "I," which is why I've assigned this Memory Palace to myself).

Notice that nearly every Memory Palace belongs to the house of a friend. Wherever possible, I have associated the sound of the letter with the sound of the friend's name. This is a memorization trigger. If

I forget that Л has an "l" sound, then it's a simple matter of recalling that I've assigned it to Lyle's house to remember that, and vice versa.

However, if you have gone through the previous exercise of building a Memory Palace to learn and store the entire Russian alphabet, forgetting individual letters and how they sound shouldn't be a problem. Nonetheless, associating the Memory Palaces you will assign to each letter effectively "compounds" the knowledge in your mind (see the chapter on compounding for more ways to use this technique).

Next, send a message to learnandmemorize@zoho.com for your Magnetic Memory worksheets. These will help you develop at least 10 stations within each of the Memory Palaces you've just assigned to locations that you are very familiar with.

As always, design your journey from station to station in such a way that you do not cross your own path and that you do not trap yourself. Always leave yourself with the ability to add another 10 stations in each location.

For some letters, you may need up to 500 stations or more in order to achieve boosts of fluency in Russian. If you find it difficult to imagine how you could ever come up with 500 stations or more in a single Memory Palace, subscribe to the free newsletter and discover dozens of ideas that will show you how (in addition to the ideas found throughout this book).

Here's a very important point: As you are trying to come up with each location to link with each letter, let yourself relax. Your mind has the perfect associations for you, so long as you don't force it. If you can't think of something that is totally fitting, such as Frank's Apartment for **Ф**, just let your mind do its work and go with whatever feels right. You do not want odd or awkward associations that cause you to stumble in your thinking. You want the associations to be natural so that you can move fluidly through your mind when searching for the words you have remembered.

Obviously, the need for relaxation will be the same for anyone. When it comes to speaking and understanding what you hear or read, you will often need to do this in real time. It is therefore important not to hinder your progress by using forced associations that you will forget or struggle to work your way back to. That will take the fun out of everything. We relax while memorizing to train ourselves to relax during recall. It's pure Pavlovian conditioning, but it works.

Now, to demonstrate how you can build out each Memory Palace location by creating a journey of at least 10 stations, let me demonstrate with the Russian letter **П**.

For **П**, which is my friend Paul's house, my first ten stations for Russian vocabulary are:

1. Pauls's room (terminal location)
2. Upstairs bathroom
3. Staircase
4. Living room
5. Dining Room
6. Kitchen
7. Front entrance closet
8. Front entrance guest bathroom
9. Front Entrance
10. Driveway

What I've done here is select a terminal location within the house and then worked my way out to the driveway. This means that I do not have to cross my path and will not get trapped. Once I've used these ten stations, I can easily add another ten, assuming that my memory of the short walk to the subway system is strong. I could also skip to the subway system if need be, and from there I have a strong memory of all kinds of stops that can be used for storing words.

Of course, using the principles of preparation and predetermination, you will have carefully assessed the suitability of your Memory Palace for this letter before starting to use it.

Before continuing, let me note that two of the keys to success with the Magnetic Memory system are working alphabetically and word division. These procedures mean that we memorize words in groups based on, not just the first letter of the word, but also the first two, three or four letters.

In the case of Russian, for example, there are numerous words that begin with **П** followed by **ос**.

By creating a Memory Palace journey that focuses just on words that start with **Пос**, we give ourselves an extra mnemonic device. We will never struggle to remember how exactly a certain word starts, because we know several things:

1. We know that the word is in our **П** Memory Palace.

2. We know that it is in the **Пос** area of the journey.

Another thing that word division allows us to do is create "bridging images." For example, **Пос** could remind you of a posse, allowing you to associate each and every word that starts with **Пос** with a posse of gangsters. By doing so, we essentially create yet another aid to memorization.

Thus, focusing on **Пос** words maximizes the memorization while limiting the potential for confusion. Were we to clump random words together, we would need to remember which word came next blindly, or at least without some form of arbitrary connective tissue. However, when we know that there are a number of **Пос** words and place them in order, doing so aids and strengthens the associations. It also assists recall for reasons that will become clear.

But for now, in the example that follows, I have greatly simplified my memorization by choosing to simply move from one **Пос** word to the next in alphabetical order. I do not have to struggle with remembering what will come next.

The first **Пос** word I would like to learn is **посерёдке**. This word means either "in the middle" or "halfway along."

To remember that **посерёдке** means "in the middle," I place a posse of gangsters in Paul's bedroom. I have the posse in the middle of the room cutting an asteroid in half. The "asteroid" helps trigger the sound of the second half of the word while also giving me a clue as to its meaning.

Moving on, I want to learn **посёрть**. Following my carefully prepared and predetermined journey through this Memory Palace, I will place **посёрть** in the upstairs bathroom of Paul's house. This word is used to describe the process of something becoming or growing a dark grey color. I see a posse of gangster clowns in Paul's shower. They are washing away all their beautiful rainbow colors, revealing their dark grey skin underneath. As always, the image is large, exaggerated and vibrant – even the grey is exaggerated.

For our next example, **посидёть** means to sit for a little while. On the staircase in Paul's house I see a posse of gangsters sitting down. To make the image more memorable, I see each of the gangsters holding a hatchet in a threatening manner.

There are many more example palaces coming up later on in this book. I have given these few examples for now to get you started on thinking about the possibilities that await you on your journey towards greater fluency with the Russian language. Remember: carefully plan your journey in advance, assign a Memory Palace to a single letter, focus on word division and "bridging images" (such as the posse that I carried from station to station in order to help create memorable continuity) and always make sure to exaggerate everything.

As ever, always look for ways to adapt these methods to your own style and comfort. If any of the images or short vignettes I suggest work for you, by all means use them. However, in my experience, each of us needs to take the principles and create our own images. The more the associative material comes from within your mind using your own creativity, the more memorable the target words will be for you. Just make sure to always use exaggeration and action in combination with location. Focus on vibrant and zany associations within carefully selected Memory Palaces that do not require any effort from you in order to make a journey from a terminal location, one that never requires you to cross your own path or become trapped. This is the key to experiencing success with this method.

What To Do If You Struggle With Memorizing The Russian Alphabet

Although I find it unlikely that anyone who uses a Memory Palace following the principles laid out in this book should have a difficult time memorizing the Russian alphabet, there is an alternative option if you do.

This option involves "translating" or "transliterating" the Russian alphabet into the Latinate alphabet.

It also means creating, not 33, but 26 Memory Palaces. This is because when you transliterate Russian into English, you are using the Latinate alphabet to render the words.

Luckily, there is an online tool designed for the purposes of automatically translating Russian letters into our alphabet:

http://www.lexilogos.com/keyboard/russian_conversion.htm

(Thanks go to one of the readers of my Magnetic Memory newsletter for bringing this website to my attention. If you're reading this, you know who you are and have my gratitude!)

One of the things you can do with this website is enter entire words.

Take **посидéть** for example. Once entered into this website, it is rendered as *posidét'*. Likewise, **посерёдке** is automatically rendered as *poserëdke*.

This is a tremendously powerful tool to use while learning and memorizing Russian because you can essentially use it to do the "homophonic transliteration" for you.

In other words, instead of figuring out how each and every word sounds by translating them letter for letter, you can pop entire words into this website and get an immediate rendering in the Latinate alphabet.

You still need to be careful that you have correctly understood the pronunciation, but you're in a perfect position now to pop Russian vocabulary into Memory Palaces based, not on the Russian alphabet, but the English alphabet instead. Either way, you've got a powerful means of memorizing all the words you wish.

What About Memorizing Gender?

This book does not purport to teach the memorization of Russian grammar. However, I do have a few tips for the easy memorization of genders.

In my memory palaces, I associate all masculine nouns with a boxer, all feminine nouns with a skirt and all neutral nouns with fire.

For example, typically words that end in consonants are masculine. Thus, to memorize that **год**, which means "year," is masculine, it would be a simple matter of seeing a calendar jumping around in a boxing ring wearing boxing gloves.

Words that end with ь on the other hand, tend to be feminine, so a word like **голова**, (head, mind, brains) could be memorized as feminine by having a giant brain wearing a skirt.

Words that end in о or е tend to be neuter, so it is a simple matter to see an **окно**, or window, on fire when you place the word in the appropriate Memory Palace.

Another Method for Storing Gender

To be as complete as possible, here's an idea I have

heard several people talk about over the years. This procedure has never worked for me, because I find it too messy. It involves throwing words "into the void," as someone once called it, which is to say, using associative imagery without organizing the associations in a carefully planned and predetermined organizational Memory Palace.

Nonetheless, the fact that it hasn't proved useful to me does not mean you won't find a way to use it. A very important principle of the Magnetic Memory system is that we are always flexible to other approaches, or at the very least, strive to recognize that they exist.

If you want to try this method, here's how it works: Instead of having gender nouns stored in palaces based around the alphabet, some people pick a city and use it as one large Memory Palace. They then divide the city into three parts: masculine, feminine and neutral.

Conclusion

To conclude this chapter, here is a list of action steps for immediate implementation on your journey toward memorizing vocabulary, regardless of the language:

1. Don't do anything until you've fully and clearly understood how to use location, imagination and action in order to effectively memorize at least ten items.

2. Take your time creating the individual locations and stations within the locations. It will take between 1-5 hours to come up with 33 locations and at least 10 stations within each location, but you can speed up the process by being relaxed while you create. Your mind has everything that you need, so long as you can push your critical mind aside and let your creative mind work. Please realize that it is not absolutely necessary to devise all 33 palaces straight away. But I prefer that my memory students have all 33 set up in advance so that they are ready to pop new words in without thinking about the process when they want to memorize a word, but I know that some people want to focus more selectively on just the letters A through H. Such deliberate focus is perfectly fine too. Whether your choose to complete all 33

letters or just a portion of the alphabet, email learnandmemorize@zoho.com now for your free Magnetic Memory Worksheets. They will literally do all the work for you.

3. Ensure that your journey in each and every Memory Palace can be undertaken without crossing your own path or getting trapped. It is tempting to think that one can get away with circling around the forward trajectory of a path, but in the long run, this will only confuse matters. Strive for clear, crisp and direct journeys so that you don't need to think about what belongs where. Remember, the fewer things you have to remember, the easier it will be to recall the vocabulary words you have placed in palaces.

4. Use Word or Excel or a handwritten document for each Memory Palace. Start with the first location and proceed linearly from there. Don't forget that the purpose of this part of the process is twofold. First, preparing a written record will help you build your memory palaces with much greater detail than doing it in your imagination alone. Second, your written record will allow you to test the words you have placed in your mind.

5. Examine the grammatical variations of the words you've chosen to place in your palace. Will you need to remember the

gender? Is it a verb that will need declension? Allow your imagination to take the principles you have been learning from this book and show you the best imagery for memorizing these different structural elements of any given word. Use relaxation to facilitate the process.

6. At the risk of being repetitive, please make sure that you are using the location, imagination and action principles. I mentor many people and a significant number of them report or demonstrate that they've fallen back on rote learning. They are repeating the words to themselves again and again rather than engaging the system I've taught them. Believe it or not, but both the mind and the body find this very stressful, contributing to fight or flight responses, frustration and ultimately failure. Future chapters describe a number of supplementary exercises that you can use to train your memory in greater depth if you feel that you need more training. I can tell you that if I hadn't gone through those exercises myself, I never would have devised the 33-letter Memory Palace system in the first place, let alone developed any skill with acquiring a second and third language. They may not seem related, but think of it as the relationship between push-ups and boxing. Pushing the floor away from the body is one of the best ways to

strengthen your punch, even though it's a completely different movement.

7. Learn the genders of every word right away. Decide upon what will signify masculine and feminine and use them consistently. This will become second nature. You don't have to use a boxer and a skirt. Go with whatever your imagination brings to you naturally.

8. Decide upon a focus. I recommend that you make adjectives a priority. Nouns and verbs are great and you will need them, but adjectives allow you to flavor your speaking and deepen your understanding of innuendo and metaphor. When you do work with verbs, pick strong verbs and learn more than one version of each (instead of just "run," also learn "jog" and "sprint"). As for nouns, use a Visual Dictionary to find your words. This will help you be more selective in the words you choose and give your imagination more fodder for making memorable associations.

9. Sit with a dictionary as often as possible. When you have worked out your 33-letter Memory Palaces in advance, you are literally going to siphon the dictionary into your mind. Although many words may fail to capture your interest, there is no need to fight with them. Simply find the words that interest you the most or that you think will be the most useful and focus on them.

Even if you skip a dozen words in a row, you can always go back to them. Focus on steady progress rather than being a completionist. Never allow frustration to enter the picture.

10. Many words you will encounter can mean several things at once. Focus on just one meaning at a time. You can always go back to gather more meanings (see the chapter on compounding).

11. Go to the library, Netflix, YouTube or a store that sells DVDs and stock up on programs in the target language. Mixing Memory Palaces with as much immersion as possible will make for great strides in your learning. Likewise, learners can listen to audiobooks, read comics, seek out bilingual editions of novels and listen to music in Russian. There are endless possibilities and you will be glad that you have taken this extra step.

12. Be careful that the images you use actually help you remember the meanings of the words. It's a painful experience to have installed familiarity with the sound and spelling of a word, only to forget what it means. It's one thing to remember that "epanadiplosis" has something to with an anaconda in your Memory Palace, but if you can't remember that it refers to the repetition of the first word of a sentence at the end of the sentence, then time, effort

and energy has been lost. Please see the following chapter on compounding for additional ideas on how to make sure you never forget the meanings of the words you have learned.

Note: Although I advocate sitting with a dictionary and memorizing key words in alphabetical order, not everyone does. And admittedly, some interesting ideas emerge.

Anne Merit, for example, talks about "clustering" words in an article she wrote for *The Telegraph* (see the resources section for a link to the article). She points out that one risks being "all over the place" by using word-a-day email services because so many themes get mixed together.

Her proposed solution is to gather together "clusters" of related words. For example, you could focus on words related to health, education, a particular sport or any particular category you like that is thematically related.

My response to this notion is that it is not only a great idea, but one that gels with the alphabetical Memory Palace technique taught in this book. Using this approach, all the memorizer needs to do is gather together words based on a theme that start with the same letter and then place them in palace accordingly.

Conversely, one can gather thematically related words that do not start with the same letter, and still divide them into your predetermined locations based on their alphabetical order.

For myself, my goal is to memorize the entirety of the languages I study, and even if I don't memorize all the words, reading through one or more dictionaries deeply familiarizes a person with the language in ways that listening to television and watching radio never will. (Okay, "listening to television and watching radio" is a ridiculous Spoonerism, but I reversed their order just to see if you're awake!)

My own preferences aside, as mentioned in the introduction, the key to memorization is to take the basic techniques and always remain alert to opportunities to expand and improve them. Your fluency – and your exercise-hungry brain – will thank you for it every day for the rest of your life.

CHAPTER THREE: NOTES ON THE CREATION AND MANAGEMENT OF RUSSIAN LANGUAGE MEMORY PALACES

Russian vocabulary is most rapidly acquired by learners who come to the task prepared with the necessary number of Memory Palaces. We've already talked about some of the points covered in this chapter, but I want to devote a special section to creating and maintaining the palaces in order to add depth and detail to the process. The more time you spend now on understanding the concept involved, the more time you'll have later to focus on acquiring Russian vocabulary with ease.

Each of your locations should have at least 10 stations to begin with, each prepared and ready to be populated with association-rich images that will bring the words you have learned easily to mind whenever you need them. As ever, your Memory Palaces should be constructed in such a way that you will never cross your own path or reach a dead end.

Keep in mind that you always want to be able to add more stations. It is unlikely that you will ever need more than 100 in any given palace, but if ever you do, you should be prepared to have places to add them.

Some people tell me that it is impossible for any given palace to have so many stations. However, if you think of all the places you've lived, it will quickly become clear to you that the possibilities are endless. If you can squeeze just 10 stations out of your current home by using individual rooms and doorways, then with a little thought, you can extend that to twenty.

What route takes you to the bus stop? Surely there are numerous memorable locations on the way: the bakery, the florist, the dental clinic above the hearing loss centre. If you take the subway, each stop can become it's own station where you leave an image. For years I have used both the Toronto, New York and Berlin subway systems as Memory Palaces and each provide countless stations where I can leave words that I want to remember for easy recall.

Remember: *preparing and predetermining your locations and stations in advance is of the utmost importance when it comes to rapidly acquiring a large vocabulary. Please spend the time to create your constellation of palaces before placing even a single word of Russian vocabulary into your mind.*

The next matter of importance is relaxation. Please see the final chapter for detailed information about creating the perfect mental and physical state for vocabulary acquisition.

Next is the matter of maintenance. At the risk of being repetitive, I have included this information twice in this book. As we all know, the Russian alphabet has 21 letters. Our months have either 29, 30 or 31 days in them. This means that you will always have plenty of time for rehearsal.

Although the memorization of vocabulary using the system taught in this book has lasting power, it is important to perform "quality control." This means revisiting the words you have memorized at least once a month. It's easy enough to do: you know where you keep all your words beginning with the letter A, so it's just a matter of wandering through the palace.

I schedule monthly maintenance sessions loosely based on the number of palaces. Take November, which has 30 days. Day 1 is dedicated to the letter A, Day 2 to the letter B and so forth. If there is a letter with a large number of words I have memorized (some of my letter palaces have 100-200), I assign more than 1 day to wandering through those particular palaces.

Taking such steps is well worth the effort and the exercise also strengthens your familiarity with the language because you begin to see patterns in the language you are studying. As previously mentioned, the more you use Russian to memorize Russian, the better.

CHAPTER FOUR:
HOW TO EXTEND MEMORY RETENTION USING COMPOUNDING EXERCISES & GENERATE EXCITEMENT FOR LEARNING RUSSIAN VOCABULARY

This chapter will be useful for anyone memorizing Russian vocabulary, but especially for those who need to learn the language for purposes other than pleasure. Many professionals learn Russian for entrepreneurial purposes or for work. Without true passion behind the enterprise, even the simple technique of using memory palaces can seem drab and unexciting. There is hope and this chapter will put you in control of how you approach your memorization sessions.

Generating Excitement

In one of his information products devoted to helping people optimize their mental processes, Mike Koenigs talks about speed-reading. For him, one of the best methods for reading a book quickly is to pretend that you will be interviewing the author on live television the next day. Millions of viewers will be watching, which means that you'll need to know the book very well, with both depth of understanding about the message and accuracy about the specific details of the content.

I think Koenigs' idea is brilliant and very adaptable to memorizing vocabulary. When I am heading to events, parties or professional opportunities where I know I will need more vocabulary on hand in order to maximize the potential benefits of the occasion, I create urgency and excitement by pretending that *I* am going to be interviewed. When learning and memorizing new Russian vocabulary, for example, I pretend that I have a book to sell that has been translated into Russian and know that people are only going to want to own it forever if I am able to win their hearts by speaking to them intelligently. To amp things up, I sometimes pretend that a movie deal is in the works, but only if I can convince the producer that I know enough Russian to consult on the screenplay and production.

There are many motivational tricks like this that

anyone can use to get themselves excited if they don't naturally feel motivated to learn and memorize the vocabulary of their target language.

Compounding

When revisiting words, you will sometimes discover that you cannot perfectly recall certain words and their meanings. You feel sure that your images are vibrant, well-located and buzzing with action and energy. Yet, when you look for the words, you still struggle to recall them.

This can lead to stress and anxiety because you know that without being able to call them to mind easily and effortlessly, you are going to be self-conscious about struggling when speaking or taking a test and the thought of stress alone will make you even more self-conscious.

Relax. Refuse to be frustrated or concerned because this is simply an opportunity to compound your memorizations.

Many of my students feel that they want to replace the original images they've created, but I caution against this because that can leave "fossils" that will only confuse matters later.

Instead, add to the image and enhance it. Take the following example: The word for "to help" in Russian is "aider." If you were to use Yoda helping the magician Michael Ammar across a street on the Death Star to memorize this word, but still could not produce "aider," then you would need to compound the image by either making it more vivid in your mind or adding something to increase its "stickiness." Perhaps Ammar has "help" tattooed on his forehead, or better yet, is screaming for help because someone is branding the word "help" on his forehead. There is always a way to compound images to make them more memorable.

Please realize that there is nothing wrong with your mind if you find weaknesses in your new 21-letter Memory Palace systems. It's just a matter of going back and compounding the images. In most cases, a second pass will do the trick. Any more than three passes suggests that you need to go back and review the central tenants of the techniques taught in this book. Avoid rote learning at all costs.

In addition, you might like to compound and reinforce the Memory Palaces themselves. If your memory of some locations is not as strong as you originally thought, then you may want to work with another location altogether. This happened to me recently when I wanted to use my old senior high school. I did my preparatory work and predetermined 20 separate stations. However, when placing new words, I found that I kept forgetting the next station in line after the first eight stations were used up.

This lack of familiarity became such a barrier that I needed, not to scrap the palace, but use it for another letter. I chose K because there are only a handful of words that begin with that letter and I could place them in a part of the palace that I definitely knew very well.

Ultimately, the amount of time spent on rehearsing, compounding and "renovating" depends on the level of experience and general enthusiasm for memorization. Again, make sure that you complete the preparation and predetermination exercises as fully as possible. Giving them their full attention will save you plenty of time and sweat later. But when leaks in the system do occur, no stress. Simply wander through your palaces and make "repairs."

CHAPTER FIVE:
EXAMPLE MEMORY PALACE FOR THE LETTER A

When picking locations for your Memory Palaces, it's best to simply relax and allow your mind to find the perfect place. When I worked on the letter A in Russian, my mind thought instantly of my friend Alan's house. Although I've only visited him there a few times, our minds have a keen ability to remember the layouts of buildings, so it was therefore very easy to through and chart out a number of locations for placing Russian vocabulary words.

Notice that A is associated with Alan. This isn't necessary. You can go with whatever location your mind brings you. In general, however, if you can come up with something bears a natural association with the location in question, such as starting with the same letter – either in visual shape or its sound – you will automatically strengthen the memorization efforts you make.

What follows are some of the stations in my A(lan) Memory Palace, the words I have placed there and a description of the images and actions I used to learn and memorize the words.

As described in an earlier, I like to group words together using the principle of "word division," especially when beginning with a new language. This allows me to create a "bridging image" that serves as an additional memory aid.

In the examples that follow, I will focus only on words that begin with "AB" to illustrate this principle. By making this selection for this specific Memory Palace journey, I am able to use a famous figure to structure my journey through the various locations. The figure I use for "AB" words is Abraham Lincoln. I chose him because, when you think about it, he is already strange and memorable – especially in a Memory Palace devoted to Russian! The zany images I can create by using him will definitely be strange and memorable because Lincoln will always be completely out of context.

To remind myself that in Russian, B sounds as "V," Lincoln is wearing a huge "V" shaped hat in each and every image.

1. Main bedroom: **аванс**. This word means "advance," as in money given in advance. It's very similar to the English word, but to bring out the distinction, I see Abraham Lincoln dancing on a van. Because this word is a masculine noun, Lincoln is wearing boxing gloves while he dances.

2. Bathroom: **авантюрист.** This word means "knight of fortune," or perhaps what we would now call a "soldier of fortune." It sounds rather similar to "adventurous," in English, but with a strong "avant-yoo-reest" sound. To memorize this word, I see Abraham Lincoln pouring an enormous sack of baking yeast into the tub.

3. Laundry room: **авантюра.** This is the word for "gamble," and seems to be cognate with the English word "venture." Since it sounds like "avant-jur-ah," I see Abraham Lincoln stuffing Ace Ventura Pet Detective into the washing machine.

4. Kitchen entrance: **аварийный.** This word means "wreckage" and sounds something like "avareen-ee." To memorize it, I see Abraham Lincoln with the actor Ben Vereen. He is on his knees proposing marriage.

5. Kitchen stovetop: **авиапочта**. This word means airmail and sounds like it: ah-via-po-chta. To memorize it, I see Abraham Lincoln opening up his eyes and poaching the contents on the stovetop while an aviator circles around his head.

Before moving on to the next sample Memory Palace, I would like to offer a note on the use of extreme imagery: I recently received a criticism from a reviewer of one of my language memorization books regarding the aggressive nature of the images I suggest. I really appreciate the feedback from my readers, and responded by explaining that I personally use violent images in a cartoonish way because it is a proven method of enhancing recall. However, people who feel sensitive in this regard should experiment with other ways of amplifying their images.

As I have repeatedly indicated, when approached like a bicycle, these techniques truly have universal application. But everyone needs to adjust every new bike they ride in order to achieve maximum results, not to mention maximum pleasure during each and every ride. Experiment with what works for you and discard the rest – or rather saving what isn't working now in your arsenal. You never know when the material will come in handy.

CHAPTER SIX:
EXAMPLE MEMORY PALACE FOR THE LETTER Ж

In this Memory Palace, I have once again picked a specific kind of word to work on: Russian words that start with the letters "ЖА." The first thing that comes to mind to help me organize "ЖА" words is Jack Nicholson as the Joker in Tim Burton's *Batman*. I find this association particularly appealing because so many different crazy images can be generated from this character. Also, notice that following the principle of compounding, the "Ja" in "Jack" and the "J" in "Joker" help concentrate the fact that this letter is the equivalent of "J" in English and usually makes the same manner of sound. This sound can also be represented as "z."

Before continuing with the demonstration, I want to point out that I have charted my journey through this Memory Palace so that I never cross my path, nor do I wind up getting trapped. This is a key component of the Magnetic Memory system.

Dining room table: **жадный**. Pronounced like "zjad-knee" or "zad-knee" this word means greedy or covetous. It's a simple matter to see the Joker greedily trying to steal Batman's "knee."

Kitchen counter: **жажда**. Sounding like "zazda," this word means "wish." Since it's a feminine noun, I see the Joker wearing a skirt and dancing around shouting "when you wish upon a da da da …"

Fridge: **жаждущая**. Sounded as "zazdusaja," this word means "solicitous," so I see the Joker knocking on the fridge with a "saw." The fridge is also now the door of a lawyer (i.e. a solicitor). "

Kitchen entrance: **жадная**. Pronounced "zadna-ya," this word means "ravenous." I see the Joker with Batman's knee again. This time he's biting into it as a huge, vibrant comic thought-bubble blinks: "gnaw-ya, gnaw-ya."

CHAPTER SEVEN:
EXAMPLE MEMORY PALACE FOR THE LETTER ф

I will use my friend Frank's apartment house for the letter ф.

As always, I have started at the back of the palace and moved forward to prevent myself from getting trapped. I also make sure that I never cross my path in order to avoid confusing myself.

Finally, to speed my progress in learning, I pick a particular kind of ф word, in the case of this example, "фаг" words. I do this because it allows me to pick an image that can carry across a number of different stations in the ф Memory Palace.

In this case, I'm going to demonstrate for you a "switch" from one word type to another. Assume that I have already memorized a number of "фаг" words using a cigarette (because "fag" is slang for cigarette in some parts of the English-speaking world). Watch how this works when I switch from one word time to another within a single Memory Palace:

Guest bedroom: **фагот**. Pronounced "fah-goat," this is the Russian word for "bassoon." I see Frank playing an enormous cigarette in the shape of a bassoon. To compound the memorization, I here Frank playing the bassoon part in Edvard Grieg's *In the Hall of the Mountain King* through this bizarre, bassoon-shaped cigarette. Because this word is masculine, Frank is wearing huge, vibrant, colorful boxing gloves as he plays. And he is kind of punching the instrument as he plays it in order to help make the image as strange as possible.

At this point, we're going to switch from "фаг" words to "фаз" words. This is as simple as imagining Frank putting down the cigarette and picking up a phaser from the Star Trek series of TV shows and films (every body knows how to set their phasers to stun, right?)

Guest bedroom entrance: **фазировать**. Fittingly enough, this word means "to phase." It sounds like "fazirovat'." To memorize it, I see Frank using the phaser to stun a "vat" of bubbling acid standing in the entrance to the guest bedroom.

As you can see, it's easy to make the transition between word types simply by using the principle of word division to make a "switch."

CHAPTER EIGHT: BUILDING FOCUS AND OVERCOMING PROCRASTINATION FOR THE ACHIEVEMENT OF FLUENCY

I've had many students approach me and say, "This is fantastic. I've been working at this and regularly memorize over a hundred words in a day. But what I don't really know is which words should I be focusing on in order to see the greatest improvement when it comes to fluency?"

This question is very good and very important. One of the first things a person can do is pop the phrase: "100 most important words in Russian" into Google. You can also search for "Russian word frequency." Doing this will give you plenty of lists from which to build a learning strategy.

But students also often complain that they cannot focus, or haven't the will power to spend the necessary time on vocabulary acquisition. To address this problem, here are a few points about learning and concentration that I have picked up over the years. A more sophisticated understanding of these concepts will make for better Memory Palace experiences for yourself and for the people with whom you discuss this system.

One way of thinking about learning and

memorization is to see them as two different skills. However, learning a language is essentially memorizing its words so that you can use them with ease whenever you like. Fundamentally, then, all learning is memorization and all memorization is learning. The only question lurking in between, particularly with respect to language learning, is: do you have to understand what you've remembered in order to remember it?

The answer, of course, is no. Many times I have learned a word and forgotten what it meant. As discussed in a previous chapter, this is why compounding images and rehearsal or revisiting the palaces frequently is so important.

However, there are some barriers that prevent us from taking these important steps. One of the biggest impediments is procrastination. We all procrastinate, and this is just something for the sake of sanity that we have to admit to ourselves. Since we all do it, there is really nothing to be gained from punishing ourselves or feeling bad about our procrastination. The fact of the matters is, that sitting around feeling bad for doing nothing inevitably leads to more sitting around doing nothing. It makes the problem worse.

The author Tim Ferris, who made his claim to fame with books such as *The 4 Hour Workweek* and *The Four Hour Body* discusses a very interesting method for dealing with procrastination. He allows it to happen. He knows it is inevitable, so he plans for it. One of the best quotes I've heard from him is that we should "budget for human nature instead of trying to conquer it."

Why am I telling you this? The reason is because in order to develop a substantial vocabulary in Russian, you are going to need to spend some time. Although it really will take you only between 1-5 hours to build a full set of alphabetical palaces, filling them with Russian vocabulary is another matter. When learning a second language, depending on your goals, you can literally spend a lifetime still developing your Memory Palaces. That said, I have had people regularly tell me about learning 100 words in under an hour. As with any skill, concentrated focus and dedicated practice wins every time.

Despite my own achievements, when I sit down to read a sophisticated novel in German or Spanish, I need to put in some time extending my Memory Palaces and inserting new words. I do this before reading, during reading and after reading. Flipping through the book I always finds words I don't know, and so make a point of jotting these down, looking them up and memorizing them. I am always pleased when I come across them again and know what they mean. I do this first because I like to keep moving forward when reading.

When I do encounter words I don't know, I pause only to keep lists for future memorization sessions. However, I try to practice what Dan Sullivan calls "speed of implementation." The sooner I place the words I've learned within the organizational model of my memory palace after encountering them in my reading, the better I remember the context in which I have learned them. Memorization from the dictionary alone is great, but remembering words encountered in normal prose has a special effect precisely because you have the aura of context to draw upon.

Returning to procrastination, the point is that we mustn't punish ourselves for skipping a few days here and there. As Ferris suggests, we will do much better over the long haul if we routinely schedule the days we miss. Intentional procrastination can even be inspirational because as you are working, you know that some vegetation-time on the couch is just waiting for you enjoy.

Four Ways to Choose the Words You Learn

The next issue is word selection. It is important to know what kinds of words one wants to memorize, particularly in the beginning. There are four guidelines that you can use:

1. Examine the meaning of the words. This is a rather obvious point, but it is an important step to take because there are some words that you may not need to memorize right now. As well, it is important to pay attention to the grammatical function of the word. Verbs and adjectives may take more importance than nouns at particular times in your progression towards fluency. You might want to spend a month with each word type, for example. By excluding word categories, you can often learn more over the long run, and also a lot more about the language itself and how it works.

2. You should ask yourself: why is it that I want to know this particular word? Do I need the word for a particular meeting I'm going to or to understand a book I'm reading? Have I noticed it in the Russian newspapers or magazines I've been glancing at? These are all important questions. You might also ask if the word is a synonym of other words you already know. You should always be interested in learning synonyms. I recommend that all language learners invest in a thesaurus in the language they are studying.

3. Consider how the word will be used in a sentence. If you cannot immediately think of how the word would be used, then search for an example using either an online dictionary or a print dictionary that comes

with complete sentence examples. It's always worth learning words even if you haven't got a feel for how to use them. When working to overcome procrastination, you will feel that much more progress has been gained by learning words that you know can be put into practice with greater immediacy.

4. You can inspire yourself by thinking about what you'll be able to achieve by having this new word firmly ensconced in your mind. This is a wonderful way to find motivation for learning

5. For more valuable tips on breaking the procrastination habit, join the Magnetic Memory mailing list by sending a message to learnandmemorize@zoho.com. A wealth of free material awaits you.

CHAPTER NINE: USING RELAXATION TO AID THE MEMORIZATION PROCESS

A friend of mine suggested that I call this chapter "Relax to Rememberize," but I thought it rather too cute. "Remembercize" was another suggestions – and I ultimately cannot disagree with the connotation that remembering is a kind of exercise.

Harry Lorayne has pointed out that one of the reasons why we can't remember the names of people we meet is because we haven't paid attention to them in the first place. I believe that tension, stress and not being present gets in the way of the attention needed for Memory Palace work.

The number one reason you want to be relaxed when you learn vocabulary is because it will *train you to be relaxed when you are trying to recall the words in normal conversation*. Nothing is worse than knowing a word, but being unable to recall it due to nervousness or feeling like you are on the spot.

To that end, I want to share with you some principles of breathing that you can use while memorizing vocabulary. Since so many of us experience confidence issues around our memories, we need relaxation in order to overcome such boundaries. Fortunately, this is easily done.

The two main strategies I use have wider applications than memory work alone. I recommend using them every day for general health as well.

I know of nine breathing techniques overall, one of which I will discuss in this chapter. It is called Pendulum breathing. The second involves progressive muscle relaxation.

Pendulum Breathing

If you've ever seen a pendulum, then you know that there is an interesting moment at the end of each cycle where the pendulum seems to hang for an instant and then move a little bit more in the first direction before falling back the other way. It does this back and forth. Pendulum Breathing works much in this way.

To start with Pendulum breathing, fill your lungs normally, and then pause slightly. Instead of exhaling, breathe in a little bit more. Let the breath out naturally and pause. Instead of inhaling, exhale out a little bit more. By circulating your breath in this way, you are "swinging" the air like a pendulum. This practice will reduce stress in your overall life once you are used to doing it, but if you do nothing else, implement pendulum breathing in your memory work. This method of breathing makes Memory Palace construction and the generation of images and associations so much easier because you are putting yourself in a kind of oxygenated dream state.

At first, it may seem difficult to concentrate on both your breathing and doing imaginative Memory Palace building. In some ways, it is like being a drummer who is creating three or four different patterns, one for each limb. With practice, the ability will come to you. The best part is that this form of practice is incredibly relaxing.

Progressive Muscle Relaxation

Progressive Muscle Relaxation is relatively well-known, and yet so few people practice it. The work is simple: sit on a chair or lie down on a bed or the floor. Next:

1) Point your toes upward and hold.

2) Point your toes towards the wall and hold.

3) Flex your calves.

4) Flex your thighs.

5) Flex your buttocks.

6) Flex your stomach muscles, lower back muscles, chest and shoulders (all core muscles).

7) Flex your hands, forearms and upper arms.

8) Flex your neck, your cheeks and the muscles surrounding your eyes.

Practice Pendulum Breathing as you do this, or at least work to conjoin the flexing movements with your breathing.

Once you have achieved a profound state of relaxation and all of your 21 memory palaces have been built, sit with a dictionary or a list of the specific words you wish to remember and their meanings. If isolating the terms helps you, prepare an index card for each word.

As mentioned in a previous chapter, I recommend that you keep an Excel file for the purposes of testing. To do this, without looking at your list, you will write down all of the words you have memorized and only then compare them against the original list.

Otherwise, avoid rote learning at all costs. Let your Memory Palace skills do the work. Compound your images when testing routines reveal weaknesses. Just as you would relax to remember, relax to test and relax to compound as well.

Again, realize that you want to practice relaxation during memorization so that you condition yourself to be relaxed when accessing the words later during conversations with others.

CONCLUSION

Next time you are out for a walk, shopping or just wandering around the house, consider the hundreds of locations you can use to build and extend your Memory Palaces. The more we pay attention to our surroundings, the more material we have to work with. As well, take every opportunity to visit places you've previously lived or gone to school. Revitalizing your familiarity with the locations you use to build your Memory Palaces is not entirely necessary, but at the very least, you should perform a mental walkthrough to ensure that you have enough material for at least the first 10 stations and ideally many more.

In addition, utilize the power of your imaginations and the images it brings you. Harness the power of coincidences such as those I related in the examples given in this book. Make sure to remember the bicycle metaphor for memory and suit the principles to your own needs by making adjustments to the system taught in this book. You should never be afraid to play around, amplify and use absurdities. Test yourself and compound when regularly or when necessary. And always, always relax when doing memory work.

You should also spend time thinking about the kinds of words you would like to learn or need to know. You should analyze how you can group different word forms together and develop your vocabulary based on the form of the language. You will see many more connections by doing this.

It goes without saying that you should speak as often as you can and practice Memory Palace recall while engaging in conversation. This means searching for words using a specific strategy, rather than casting a hook and hoping a vocabulary fish swims by and bites.

Rather, you should hold what an associate of mine named Joshua Smith calls "natural conversations." He talks about this in a book he wrote for ESL students called "Breaking Through to Fluency." "Natural conversation" means taking both the simple and complex vocabulary words you have learned out into the real world. Experience how real people in real situations use the words. Make special "memory palace field trips." You can use these excursions to find new areas to store words while you practice having "natural conversations."

Finally, teach others what you have learned about memorization skills. Talk about how you built your Memory Palaces, the techniques of location, imagery and activity. Give your friends and colleagues examples of how you've memorized specific words. Teaching others is one of the best ways to compound information that we've learned and it allows us to see other possibilities and new techniques we may have missed.

I wish you a lot of fun with these techniques and great progress with your Russian language endeavors. I would be pleased if you contacted me to let me know how you've done. If this book has helped you, please leave a review on Amazon so that others can also find their way to these skills. Remember: the more we learn, the more we *can* learn. The same is true with memory. The more you remember, the more you have learned. And learning a new language is a special achievement indeed.

ABOUT THE AUTHOR

Anthony Metivier completed his BA and MA in English Literature at York University in Toronto, Canada. He earned a second MA in Media and Communications from The European Graduate School in Switzerland while completing a PhD in Humanities, also from York. As the author of scholarly articles, fiction and poetry, he has taught Film Studies in Canada, the United States and Germany. He plays the electric bass in the Berlin-based band *The Outside*.

SECRET BONUS SECTION #1

To thank you for reading this book, I want to give you a few special bonuses. Think of this section as one of those hidden tracks some artists put at the end of their CDs.

When I teach memory skills in a live setting, I haven't got a whole lot of time to impress my students while I'm demonstrating the memory techniques discussed in this book. Let's face it: we used to live in an instant on world. Now it's a world of instant downloads. People want the skills I have to offer and they want to download them into their brains immediately.

Here's what I've come up with a routine suggested by Michael J. Lavery of Wholebrainpowercoaching.com to help create that effect. Within fifteen minutes, I teach students to recite the entire alphabet backwards. It's strange that we cannot do this naturally and equally strange that we need to go to such elaborate lengths in order to train ourselves to do it, but it's worth the effort. Saying the alphabet backwards is the equivalent of skipping rope with your brain. It sends oxygen rich blood to your brain and will wake you up any time you need a kickstarter. And it's healthier than coffee!

Having read this book, you already have the basis for how to accomplish this feat. There's actually two ways to do it.

Option One: Create a 26-station Memory Palace. Place 26 objects, one per station. The only rule is that each object must start with a letter of the alphabet in reverse order, i.e. zebra, yolk, xylophone, weathervain, etc. As with all memory techniques, the process works best if you create your own words.

Option Two: Create a highly memorable story. This method uses a linking system taught in this book. I didn't teach it because with the exception of using it to memorize the alphabet backwards, I personally don't use it. For more on the linking technique, I recommend reading any of the books mentioned in the resources section.

Here's the story that I use to memorize the alphabet backwards:

Zebras with **Y**ellow **X**ylophones ask **W**hat to a German man named **VUT** who is a **SR** (Senior) with a **Q**uestion for the **P**ost **O**ffice in **N**orthern

Minnesota, **L**ake **K**ilimanjaro where **J**esus asks **I** (me) about the **H**uman **G**rowth **F**ormula created by the **E**ducation **D**epartment of the **C**entral **B**rain **A**dministration.

I use Option One in class to teach my students how to say the alphabet backwards, but I do it in a sneaky way. I *never* tell them that the goal is to say the alphabet backwards. I simply have them first draw a memory palace for themselves with 10 stations. I give them ten words. When they are sufficiently impressed with their ability to recall the first ten words (zebra, yolk, xylophone, etc), I have them repeat the process with a second memory palace.

With another ten words down the hatch and everyone reciting all twenty words with ease, I ask one of the students to recite the words again, but this time saying only the first letter of each word. It rarely dawns on the person speaking what they are achieving, but within seconds, the rest of the class is stunned.

Five minutes later, the students have added six more words and everyone is reciting the alphabet backwards with ease. Try this for yourself. You'll love it!

SECRET BONUS SECTION #2

In this bonus I will describe to you how that I have modified the larger principles described in the previous chapter to my own purposes as part of reaching my goals of easily memorizing the vocabulary words of different languages.

Although you may not use your memory to retain poetry, the order of a deck of cards or the number of your car and seat on a train in Spain, my hope is that you'll follow my descriptions of how I put these larger principles into action and see how to apply them in your own way.

Please don't skip this bonus section. There are many important clues and ideas that your students can use on their journey towards memorizing vocabulary. These exercises were essential to me and they will be essential to you.

Poetry and Novels

I know that we're not here to learn memory tricks, but there is little that impresses people more than the ability to whip out a heap of Shakespeare off the top of your head. I'm not talking about "To be or not to be." I'm talking about the entire soliloquy.

Poetry can be difficult to remember, especially if it is unrhymed or has an unusual rhyme structure.

Take John Keats's *Ode to a Nightingale*, for example. I love the second stanza:

> O for a draught of vintage! That hath been
> Cool'd a long age in the deep-delved earth
> Tasting of Flora and the country green.
> Dance, Provencal song, and sunburnt mirth!
> O for a beaker full of the warm South!
> Full of the true, the blushing Hippocrene
> With beaded bubbles winking at the brim
> And purple-stained mouth
> That I might drink and leave the world unseen
> And with thee fade away into the forest dim

Good stuff, no?

Now, how did I memorize it? Well, as discussed in the previous chapter I started by picking a location. As it happens, I had first encountered this poem in a classroom in Winters College at York University in Toronto where I took some of my four degrees.

I remember the room where I studied the poem and the entire building very well. So that's where I started. Remember: we use places that we know precisely because we don't have to remember them. If I know where the door is in relation to the desk where I sat, then there is no need to remember that the desk is station one and the door is station too. It just happens naturally.

So let's begin. Here is how I memorized this delightful, if sad stanza from one of Keats' most heartfelt poems.

O for a draught of vintage!

I imagined myself as large and as vibrantly as possible squeezed into the tiny desk I sat in when class was in session. I saw myself drawing the word "vintage" using dark black pencil. The pencil is enormous and digs deeply into the surface of the desk like a knife. To get more action into the scene, I imagined myself working feverishly, like a mad draftsman trying to express some unspeakable secret.

That hath been
Cool'd a long age in the deep-delved earth

By the door leading out of the classroom, I pictured a fridge, and there I saw myself digging earth out of it with a shovel. I stabbed the earth deeply with the shovel and tossed the dirt into the hall.

Tasting of Flora and the country green.

Outside in the hall, I saw myself painting the

concrete wall with flowers and a green countryside. This time I was a mad painter and this time, to remember the line, I visualized myself tasting the paint.

Dance, Provencal song, and sunburnt mirth!

By the door of the next classroom down the hall, I saw myself dancing, and then kicking Ezra Pound through the bars of a prison. For reasons I won't get into, Pound is readily associated with Provencal songs by people who majored in English. Pound also went through a period in his life where he was caged beneath the sun, and according to legend he laughed at the guards a lot. So I saw him laughing at me as I kicked him, his face badly burnt by the sun.

O for a beaker full of the warm South!

For this one I had to bent the rules of reality. There is a third classroom in Winters College on that floor, and I simply imagined that it was a scientific laboratory. Inside, I imagined a mad scientist violently cracking an egg-shaped compass pointing south into a bubbling beaker. The smoke and boiling bubbles helped me remember that the South Keats speaks of is warm.

Full of the true, the blushing Hippocrene

For this image, I moved into the staircase at the end of the corridor. I imagined a blushing Hippopotamus with his mouth full of college degrees, his belly stuffed to the brim with them.

With beaded bubbles winking at the brim

This one was easy. In the basement of Winters College is a pub run for and by students. I just saw myself trying to bead the brim of a wine glass with a needle and some thread. And of course, everything was huge, vibrant and visualized with over-the-top action. For example, I wasn't just "trying" to push a needle into the glass, but stabbing at it frantically. The imagery is kind of disturbing, but that's exactly the point. That's what makes it memorable.

That I might drink and leave the world unseen

Brace yourself for more grotesque violence. To remember this, I saw myself drinking from the glass and then stabbing myself in the eyes with the needle.

And with thee fade away into the forest dim

The patio outside the pub isn't exactly like a forest, but I still used it. I populated it with trees, made it dark, and envisioned myself being guided into the forest as the entire picture dimmed out, like the ending of a film.

In truth, memorizing the passage was not a great deal of work, partly because I love the poetry. Being able to pay attention to the subtleties of the language and Keats' particular spin on the world not only helps, but creates a sense of urgency for me. I not only want to know Keats better, but I *need* to know his poetry better. This is what I tell myself. I manufacture excitement when I don't feel it naturally. Paradoxically, I combine this sense of excitement with deep relaxation when working. This combination of excitement and relaxation helps came easily to me because I just relaxed and let them come to me. In about half an hour, I was able to recite the passage with ease.

When it comes to novels, the procedure is more or less the same. But instead of memorizing individual lines, I remember important plot points and the names of characters. Character names don't necessarily have to be remembered because the novelist will use them over and over again and in many cases we'll come to identify with the characters and remember their names naturally and without any external effort.

It helps too if you understand the shapes novels tend to take. Usually there is some kind of problem or dilemma experienced by a character who is faced by something that has happened in his or her past. The dilemma then turns into a crisis that must be dealt with, followed by a strong decision and a series of actions leading to a battle or confrontation with the antagonist. There may be a moment of self-revelation during the battle that helps the character defeat the antagonist, followed by the resolution. Obviously, not every story has this exact shape, but thinking in terms of story shape can certainly help as you work on memorizing the elements of the plot.

The important thing to keep in mind is the kind of space you use. If you are memorizing 8-10 lines of poetry, then it's possible that a single room or a small apartment with several rooms will do. I usually prefer to use one room or location for this kind of work, but if you are able to compress things in your memory palace, you could imagine a bookshelf in a room you are familiar with and use each individual book as either a portal to another memory palace or as an individual signifier of what you want to remember. It's all up to you.

But when it comes to remembering the key events of a novel, make sure that you have a big enough place so that you don't run out of stations. I wouldn't want to use Winters College to remember Tolstoy's *War and Peace*, for instance, but for something like that, Broadway in Manhattan would probably do. It's a long walk from 187 where I used to live down to the southern most tip of Broadway, but I've done it, the streets are numbered and you can easily follow it in a sequence that's hard to miss.

If you are a film reviewer, or just want to memorize the plot points of the films you see, it may take some practice to get fast enough to create vibrant, memorable and active images and store them in unique locations in real-time, but it can be done. You can also take notes and then memorize these later when you can relax.

On that note, I must say it again: one of the key points in all of memory practice that no other memory book I've read mentions is that you need to make sure that you are relaxed. If you are feeling tense or running away from a mugger (which you might be on the stretch of Broadway that runs through Manhattan), these techniques probably won't have the desired effect.

I mention this mugging example for a reason. I was once the victim of an attempting mugging on Broadway in Harlem. I know the area quite well, but I cannot use it as part of any Memory Palace because of that experience. My heart always quickens when I think of that gun pointed at me. This touch of anxiety interferes with the memorization process immensely. Keep this point in mind when building your memory palaces.

Here are some action steps that you can take immediately to start practicing the memorization of poetry:

1) Pick a poem you actually enjoy. Although it is certainly possible to memorize material you could care less about, obviously for the purposes of practice, you want to enjoy "owning" the material in your head.

2) As always, make sure that you plan out in advance where you are going to store the material. Make sure that you are familiar with the locations and that you've "cleaned" them out. If you've used the location before, you might run into some trouble if memories from the past are still lurking there.

3) Work on your memory only when you are relaxed.

4) Avoid falling back on rote memory attempts. They can sneak up so easily, but are not the point of the exercise. Use the techniques of location, imagery and action.

5) Test yourself, but in a way that doesn't involve rote learning. If you make a mistake, go back and examine the imagery you've chosen. Is it strong enough? What

might you need to add in order to make it stronger?

6) Talk to someone about the efforts you are making. This is one of the best ways to solidify your results. If you can, teach them how to do what you are doing. Teaching is not only personally edifying, but it helps to make the world a better place. And remember, the more you can remember, the more you can remember.

7) Avoid using places where stressful or painful memories might interfere with the memorization process.

SECRET BONUS SECTION #3

Imagine the following scenario.

You're seated with some friends in a restaurant. You have 52 individual objects on the table. They're quite small and easily stored in your pocket. These objects can be assembled and reassembled at will. Each object has a unique set of images on the front and look virtually identical on the back. In fact, you have to turn each one over to spot the difference between one object and another.

You have the objects out on the table because your friends have been asking you exactly how you've come to have such a powerful memory. Because you know that one of the best ways to master something is to teach it to someone else, you've decided to teach them the skills you learned in this book.

But first you want to give them a demonstration.

Imagine that you ask one of your friends to reorder the objects. They can spend as much time as they like.

Once they're done, they hand the objects to you. You turn them over one at a time, look at the fronts and then turn them back over, hiding their unique features from your line of sight for the rest of the demonstration.

When you've gotten through all 52 objects, you have the objects back to your friend. To create a bit of time delay, you recite the alphabet backwards or a new poem you've recently created.

Then, you ask your friend to look at the front of the first object.

You tell him what it is.

Your proceed to the next object and then the next and the next until you've correctly named all 52.

Your friends are amazing. You feel wonderful. You are now in a position to teach.

What are these 52 unique objects you've remembered with such tremendous ease?

Yes, you've guessed it: a deck of cards.

Would you like to be able to do what I've just described? Then read on, because the techniques in this chapter involve memorizing a deck of cards. More importantly, this skill is an important step towards finessing the minds of your students for the memorization of English vocabulary.

Admittedly, effectively memorizing a deck of cards is quite complex, at least to get started. However, do the groundwork and you'll find many more applications for the raw tools you'll need to cultivate that are applicable in numerous ways, learning German being just one of them. If nothing else, setting yourself up to be able to memorize a deck of cards quickly and efficiently will give you great exercise in the discipline needed in the Preparation and Determination department.

Think about this chapter in terms of the Karate Kid. Remember the way Mister Miyagi made young Daniel-san wash cars and mop the floor. There seemed to be no purpose in it, certainly not in terms of reaching his goals with karate. Yet, when the time came to actually implement karate skills, blammo, Daniel-san had them all at hand. So please don't underestimate the power of squats and pushups, which is essentially what this chapter is all about.

All that said, let me note that I also wanted to learn how to memorize the order of a randomly shuffled deck for the purposes of doing amazing magic tricks. I wound up gaining a lot more in the process, about memory, about language and about myself. Ultimately, there's no direct way to describe how and why this process helped me with the acquisition of different vocabulary terms other than to say that I couldn't have figured out the path without taking each and every step of my particular journey. I also learned a lot about what doesn't work for me when it comes to memorizing things during this stage of my memory journey. That is why I am sharing these details with you.

And so: following the technical description of how I learned to memorize a deck of cards, I'll follow up with the example of how I use this system to memorize the seat number on my train, or anything else I might want to remember that this system can help with.

There are a number of stages in being able to memorize a deck of randomized cards quickly and effectively.

First, we need to learn a method of organizing the cards. We do this by giving each card a number.

Since there are 52 cards in the deck, we need to divide them up according to suite and then give each suite a number. I'll explain the rationale behind these numbers in a moment, but for now, let's say that:

Spade = 10

Diamonds = 30

Clubs = 50

Hearts = 80

Now let me explain why we have designated these suites with these numbers. It has to do with a numerical sound system that works like this (believe it or not, remembering this simple list of sounds is really the hardest part of the job – the rest is just a technical application of the list):

1 = ta/da

2 = na

3 = ma

4 = ra

5 = la

6 = cha/ja

7 = ka

8 = fa/va

9 = ba/pa

0 = sa

I know what you must be thinking: these memory people are nuts! Well, there is some truth to that, but let's carry on with developing the technique.

Remember that we said the Spades are assigned the number 10. The reason for this will start to become clear when you look at the following:

Ace of Spades = 11 (Toad)

2 of Spades = 12 (Tin)

3 of Spades = 13 (Dam)

4 of Spades = 14 (Tire)

5 of Spades = 15 (Tail)

6 of Spades = 16 (Dish)

7 of Spades = 17 (Tack)

8 of Spades = 18 (TV)

9 of Spades = 19 (Tape)

10 of Spades = 20 (Nose)

Jack of Spades = 21 (Nut)

Queen of Spades = 22 (Nun)

King of Spades = 23 (Enemy)

Now, we start with the Ace of Spades as the number 11 simply to give the order a nicer sequence. Since the sound for 1 is "ta" or "da," I have made the word Toad as my association for the Ace of Spades. You could come up with whatever word you like based on "ta" or "da" sounds, but I would recommend that you pick something that can be easily imagined and placed into action in some way.

Just to be clear how the sequence works, I'll point out that the 2 of Spades is "Tin" in my system because the sound for 1 is "ta" (or "da") and the sound for 2 is "na." Therefore, 12, which is the 2 of Spades could be "tan," or "dan." Surely there are other options, but "tin" has always worked well for me.

Another tip that you might find useful is to pick words that have some personal meaning if you can. 3 of Spades is "dam" for me, not only because as a card associated with 13 is "dam" a logical word, but it also reminds me of when my father worked on a huge dam-building project. He brought me out there a few times, and to my childlike imagination, it was amazing to see the scope of that project. In fact, I think it would probably seem pretty amazing to anyone of any age. The point here is that the more personal the image is, the more staying power it has.

Now, assuming you have this system in place, let me briefly explain why after the 9 of Spades, we switch from words that start with "t" or "d" to words that start with "n." The reason is that the 9 is represented as the 19th card in the sequence, and since 1 is "ta" and 9 is "pa," I have chosen the word "tape." The Jack of Spades, however, is the 20th card. Since 2 is a "na" sound and 0 is a "sa" sound, I have selected the word "nose."

Before I give you my personal keywords for the rest of the deck, let me give you a quick example of how I would use this system just using a single suite. Let's say that I want to remember that the 9 of Spades comes on top of the 3 of Spades in a stack I am trying to memorize. I would imagine a giant role of tape manically wrapping up a huge concrete dam. Later, when I wanted to remember which order the two cards came in, it would simply be a matter of remembering the absurd image of a roll of tape crazily unraveling over the surface of a dam, as if to secure it from cracking apart in an earthquake. In fact, in order to really make it memorable, I might want to add a detail like that.

This is called "giving the association a reason." If there is a reason, no matter how absurd, that a role of tape is wrapping up a large concrete structure, then it can help with remembering it.

Let's carry on to see how I've portioned out the Diamonds using this system. Since the Diamonds fall under the number 30, most of this suite will start with "m" words. But as in every suite, we eventually come to the next group of 10, which means that the 10 of diamonds will start with an 'r' word.

Ace of Diamonds = 31 (Maid)

2 of Diamonds = 32 (Man)

3 of Diamonds = 33 (Mime)

4 of Diamonds = 34 (Mare)

5 of Diamonds = 35 (Mail)

6 of Diamonds = 36 (Match)

7 of Diamonds = 37 (Muck)

8 of Diamonds = 38 (Movie)

9 of Diamonds = 39 (Map)

10 of Diamonds = 40 (Rice)

Jack of Diamonds = 41 (Rat)

Queen of Diamonds = 42 (Ran)

King of Diamonds = 43 (Ram)

Clubs:

Ace of Clubs = 51 (Lad)

2 of Clubs = 52 (Lion)

3 of Clubs = 53 (Lamb)

4 of Clubs = 54 (Lyre)

5 of Clubs = 55 (Lily)

6 of Clubs = 56 (Leash)

7 of Clubs = 57 (Lock)

8 of Clubs = 58 (Leaf)

9 of Clubs = 59 (Leap)

10 of Clubs = 60 (Cheese)

Jack of Clubs = 61 (Cheetah)

Queen of Clubs = 62 (Chain)

King of Clubs = 63 (Gym)

And finally:

Ace of Hearts = 81 (Fat)

2 of Hearts = 82 (Fan)

3 of Hearts = 83 (Foam)

4 of Hearts = 84 (Fire)

5 of Hearts = 85 (Foil)

6 of Hearts = 86 (Fish)

7 of Hearts = 87 (Fake)

8 of Hearts = 88 (Fife)

9 of Hearts = 89 (Viper)

10 of Hearts = 90 (Bus)

Jack of Hearts = 91 (Boat)

Queen of Hearts = 92 (Bone)

King of Hearts = 93 (Bomb)

These are the words I've come up with for each card using the numerical-sound system, but it's up to you to pick the words and images that work best for you.

Now, let me tell you how I put all of this together. Do you remember how I said that I sometimes have portals inside of my memory palaces that lead to unusual places? My memorized deck of cards is an example of this.

I have lived in two apartments in the capital of Germany, Berlin. I really liked my office in the first apartment and have used it a lot to memorize many things. In the mental version of that office as I have remembered it, there is a pack of red Bicycle playing cards (I just realized now that it may be from the cards that I got the idea of explaining to people that memory systems are just like bikes!)

But instead of playing cards inside that box, there is a garage. If you've seen Christopher Nolan's second Batman film, *The Dark Knight*, you'll know the kind of space I'm talking about. In that film, Batman's "Batcave" is actually a sophisticated room, open and bright with plenty of room for automobiles.

But I don't have any fancy sports cars or Batmobiles in my garage (inside a card box in an office in an apartment in Berlin). Instead, I have the first four cars I owned as a teenager. I have the cars lined up in order from the first car to the fourth car (which also happened to be the last car I ever owned before turning to transit and rental cars only).

The first car is my blue Volkswagen Beetle. It was lowered to the ground and very special to me. Too bad I wrecked it.

My second car was an orange Volkswagen Beetle. There was nothing particularly special about it, but I miss it even to this day.

My third car was a silver Ford Fiesta. A bizarre choice, but I loved it.

My fourth car was a blue Chevy Malibu.

For the purposes of this Memory Palace, each car has 13 locations, which works nicely because each suite in a deck also has 13 cards.

The locations I use are:

>The front driver's side headlight
>
>The front passenger's side headlight
>
>The engine hood
>
>The windshield
>
>The steering wheel
>
>The driver seat
>
>The passenger seat
>
>The seat behind the driver's seat
>
>The seat behind the passenger's seat
>
>The inside of rear window

> The outside of the rear window
>
> The trunk
>
> The exhaust pipe

For some people, these stations might be too closely compressed together, but this arrangement works very well for me. In general, I like my stations to be as close together as possible.

The nice thing about each car having 13 locations is that I don't feel like I have to memorize an entire deck. Instead, I only need to remember 13 cards per car. It's ultimately rather arbitrary, but it still has a psychological effect that helps the task seem less daunting.

So, taking thirteen cards, let's see what the first car might look like:

> Front driver's side headlight = 3 of Clubs (Lamb)
>
> Front passenger's side headlight = 8 of Hearts (Fife)
>
> Engine Hood = 7 of Spades (Tack)
>
> Windshield = 6 of Spades (Dish)
>
> The steering wheel = 10 of Spades (Nose)

The driver seat = Ace of Clubs (Lad)

The passenger seat = Ace of Diamonds (Maid)

The seat behind the driver's seat = Jack of Spade (Nut)

The seat behind the passenger's seat = 3 of Diamonds (Mime)

The inside of rear window = 9 of Clubs (Leap)

The outside of the rear window = 10 of Diamonds (Cheese)

The trunk = 5 of Spades (Tail)

The exhaust pipe – 5 of Clubs (Lily)

Now it's just a matter of using location, imagery and activity to weave these images together. It's actually very easy and fun.

Just imagine a lamb standing in front of the car with a fife in his mouth. In addition to the horrible music the lamb is blaring from where he is not standing in front of the passenger side headlight, tacks are firing rapidly over the hood from the fife and smashing into the dish hovering over the windshield. Pieces of shrapnel from the dish have smashed into the nose on the steering wheel, which belongs to the lad sitting in the driver's seat. He winds up sneezing all over the maid sitting in the passenger's seat and so she steals a handkerchief from Nutty Jack of Spades in the back seat who is hitting on the mime beside him. She tries to leap through the window, but crashes her head against a huge chunk of cheese and just as she is recovering, she finds herself being smashed in the face by the tail of the dog I hate, Lily.

It seems like a lot of work, and it is. But with practice, it gets faster and easier. You'll even begin to find that you don't really need all the "training wheels" I've described as much as you did in the beginning, though they will still always be there to help you and will always remain the basic foundation of how you remember the cards. The best part is that you'll find your concentration sharpening and your attention for detail widening. It's a great mental exercise that you won't regret taking up as a habit.

Plus, it will serve as an excellent part of anyone's goal of being able to effortlessly remember vocabulary.

A few notes on this chapter:

I do not use "ran" as a verb for the Queen of Diamonds. Here I am thinking of the Kurosawa movie *Ran*, which is a samurai adaptation of

Shakespeare's *King Lear*. I actually don't picture a woman here, but the old man as he is seen sitting in ceremonial dress at the beginning of the movie.

Lily, the 5 of Clubs is not a flower, but a dog a friend of mine used to have as a pet. I never liked that dog very much, which makes it all the more effective as a memory prompt, ironically.

Leap for the 9 of Clubs is the one spot where I use a verb. I would rather not have, but I couldn't find any other image that worked for me. "Lap" would be a natural choice, but since laps don't actually exist, at least not once a person is standing, it just doesn't work for me.

As a final note to this chapter, I want to tell you a little about what didn't work for me when it came to memorizing a deck of cards. The great magician Juan Tamirez gives a number of strategies. One is to sing the order of the deck as you want to learn it. Record yourself singing the order and listen to the recording again and again. This approach is perfectly fine, so long as you want to remember a pre-arranged deck that is always pre-arranged in the memorized order. Sometimes, this is my preference, since I am adept at appearing to shuffle a deck without disturbing the order of the cards.

Nonetheless, singing the order never worked for me. It amounts to learning by rote.

Another idea Tamirez gives is to arbitrarily assign both a number and an animal to each and every card. This is getting closer to the system I ultimately landed upon, but it still leads one to use rote memorization in place of a system that lets you remember the order of the cards almost instantly.

Now that I've shared with you both what has worked for me and what hasn't, let me suggest a few ...

Action steps:

1) Make the commitment to memorize the sound system for the ten digits, 0 – 9. It's very easy.

2) Apply the number sounds to the different suits in the manner described.

3) Make a word for each card using the number system. Using a written list, Word file or Excel sheet, store the words you create so that you can test your memory of them later.

4) Decide in advance where you are going to store the order of the cards you will be memorizing. Use actual locations or invent them. Since you need 52 for this exercise, it is best to think of how you can compress them into a smaller space.

5) Make sure that you are relaxed throughout this process. Training yourself to be relaxed while working on memory techniques helps with recall. You want to "anchor" the sensation of relaxation so that you know it very well. You'll instantly fall into that state of relaxation at any time you want to with dedicated practice.

6) Get out a deck of cards, shuffle it, and begin memorizing it.

7) Test everything, but always make sure that you are not falling back on rote memory. That is not the purpose of these exercises.

8) Describe the procedures that you are using to someone else. You do not need to show off. Simply explain what you are doing.

Conclusion

Finally, here is a list of further memory resources you might like to pursue. I've mentioned Harry Lorayne several times in this book, so let's start with him. *The Memory Book: The Classic Guide to Improving Your Memory at Work, at School and at Play* is a wonderful resource. Get it here:

http://memorizegermanvocabulary.com/harrylorayne

Lorayne's website is also well worth visiting:

http://www.harrylorayne.com/

If you'd like to hear a nearly 2 hour long interview with the man himself, check out *You're Only an "Aha!" Moment from Greatness* on this website:

http://www.hardtofindseminars.com/Harry_Lorayne_Interview.htm

You'll also want to read Tony Buzan. I recommend *Use Your Perfect Memory*.

http://memorizegermanvocabulary.com/tonybuzan

A recent memory book that has gotten everyone talking is Joshua Foer's *Moonwalking with Einstein:*

The Art and Science of Remembering Everything has an appearance by Tony Buzan that is a delight to read. His success with memorization skills is absolutely stunning. Here's the link:

http://memorizegermanvocabulary.com/moonwalking

Perhaps my favorite audio program is Dominic O'Brien's *Quantum Memory Power: Learn to Improve Your Memory*. He reads the book himself, making it a wonderful experience. His passion for memorization techniques really shines through.

http://memorizegermanvocabulary.com/quantummemorypower

You've probably seen Kevin Trudeau hawking his products on late night television infomercials. Don't groan, however. His *Mega Memory* is one of the best memory products I've ever encountered. He talks a lot, but in *Mega Memory*, everything he promises is right there, ready to be learned.

http://memorizegermanvocabulary.com/megamemory

From the world of magicians and mentalists, I recommend Richard Osterlind's *Easy to Master Mental Miracles*.

http://www.mymagic.com/dvd/dvd-osterlind.htm

Spread the word!

Do you like this book? Has it helped your students to memorize English vocabulary with tangible results? If so, I want to ask you to help me tell other people about it.

Since 2007 I've made my living entirely by writing and teaching. Yet, I have done very little promotion for my books (though this is currently changing). Nearly every sale has come from people passing on the good news through word of mouth. So now I'm asking YOU to please help me spread the word.

Here's how you can help.

If you have an email list of friends and contacts, why not send them a message about this book and its contents?

Discuss the book on web forums and message boards.

Print out a few relevant pages and leave them in any common area where you work or meet with people. You can print your name on the copies so that people know they belong to you and use the material to start great conversations about language memorization.

If you have friends or contacts in the press or

media, tell them about this book. They will definitely get a good story, article or feature out of it. I can easily be contacted at any time by sending a simple email to: learnandmemorize@zoho.com.

Write a review of the book and tell people where they can find it. Post your review on Amazon.

If you write guest blogs or speak on podcasts, mention how this book has helped you.

Include this book as part of your course or your next product launch. You could also invite me to be a speaker and have me offer your students individualized coaching while I'm there. Contact me for details at learnandmemorize@zoho.com

Thank you.

Anthony Metivier

ONE LAST BONUS

Here is a sample from my new "Magnetic Memory Mondays" newsletter. It goes out every Monday and is loaded with tips, resources and inspirational ideas that will help you continue improving your memory. Subscribe today by sending a blank email to learnandmemorize@zoho.com. Remember, when you subscribe I will send you a free set of Magnetic Memory Worksheets.

5 Ways to Ruin a Perfectly Good Memory

Hey Memorizers,

I've got the itch to talk about how we sometimes ruin the perfectly good memories we've worked so hard on.

I'm thinking specifically of 5 fatal mistakes learners make that cause them to leave some seriously important memorized words floating in the mist.

So let's work like David Letterman and go through these in reverse order, beginning with ...

5. Not Picking a Place for the Memory

Once upon a time, a client in my Magnetic Memory coaching program said that it wasn't necessary to "locate" his remembered words anywhere. I'm not one to argue with people because when it comes to memorizing words, phrases, terminology or longer things they're working on like poems and speeches. It's important to go with what works.

In this case, my client was working on Spanish. He told me that when he wanted to remember something like that "vaca" means cow, he simply needed to see a cow vacumming. For him, it was just a concept that floated around in the inner space of his mind.

If that works, great.

Yet, a few weeks later, I asked him, "say, what's the Spanish word for cow?"

It took him about a minute to "find" it in his mind.

That's actually not too bad, but I know it can be better. I know it can be better because people who take the time to establish a location just for "V" words are essentially creating a groove in their mind, a place that they know where to go to look for words. It's kind of like dropping a needle on a record (you do remember records, don't you?)

A common objection to using this method is: "great, but what if I can't remember that the word begins with a "V"?"

To tell you the truth, I haven't got a hard boiled answer to this question.

What I do know is that, merely by making the effort to place the letter in an alphabetically arranged "palace" in your mind (like a palace just for "V" words), your brain has paid attention to that word and done so in a very specific way.

You've magnetized that word and given it a special charge. When the time comes to find and use that word, you're much more likely to be drawn to it.

Even if you're remembering something on the fly, stick it somewhere. When I used to take the train across Germany twice every week for my research, I always memorized the wagon and seat number on my ticket so I didn't have to pull it out of my pocket every five minutes to make sure I was standing in the right spot.

Let's say it was wagon 23, seat 92. Since 2 is "tin" in my memory and 3 is a "dam," (the kind that holds back water), I would see a dam in the shape of a Campbell's soup can bursting at the seams to hold back a river of trains. I'd make it like something out of a disaster movie so that the image was large, colorful and even quite noisy.

Even though I didn't really have to, in order to strengthen the memory, I would make sure to "place" it somewhere. What better place than the train platform itself? Merely by taking that extra bit of effort to locate the image, even though I was mentally placing just right in front of me, the memory was so much stronger when I wanted to recall it. Why? Because I knew where to find it. I completely eliminated any anxiety that it might be lost (more on that when we get to memory ruination point number 2).

The take-away here, hombre, is that memorization is a lot like Real Estate: location, location, location.

4. Not Making the Associative Image Large, Colorful and Exaggerated

For a lot of people, this is a tough nut to crack.

We shouldn't blame ourselves either. I myself am a very imaginative person, but I'm not particularly visual in my imagination. I work well with concepts.

However, I've trained myself to be more visual over the years. All it takes is practice.

The funny thing is that I actually found myself "forced" to be more visual when I got a research grant to work with an Art History department in my other career as a Film Studies professor.

That's when I got the idea that people working with their memories who suffer from what I call "image deficit" should spend some time looking at books with large reproductions of art.

You don't have to spend a pile of cash on them either. It's healthy (and normal) to spend some time at the library or at a bookstore. I'll bet that in your city or town, there are even free entrance nights at your local art gallery.

The point is: you can train your brain to be more visual and you can use that training in your memory work to make your associative images brighter, more colorful and more exaggerated.

You'll also build a large pool of images from the world of art that you can reference.

Who can forget Dali's melting clock in "The Persistence of Memory," or the lone survivors in Bruegel's "The Triumph of Death"?

You can use these monumental images in your memory palaces. So look at some art books and give this method a try.

3. Not Incorporating Action Into Your Associative Images

Action is crucial. It's not only a means of exaggerating your images, but motion captures the eye - including the mind's eye. We tend to remember the details of exactly how something happened very well, and so we need to take advantage of this mental blessing.

Sometimes readers complain about the fact that I advocate using cartoon violence in memorization work. As always, my answer is: use whatever works for you. If sunshine and daisies waving in the wind on your front deck remind you that "dactylomegaly" means an abnormal largeness of fingers and toes, then by all means use it.

However, many people will probably find that enormous daisies with huge muscles bearing hammers are pounding on your toes and making them swell into a state of "abnormal largeness" is much more memorable.

Either way, it's a mistake not to incorporate action into your memory work.

2. Not Revisiting and Rehearsing

Think about memorizing vocabulary or terminology or facts like playing music. Maybe you can "get" the song merely by looking at the sheet music once, but chances are that you'll need to play it a dozen or more times to become proficient and possible dozens more to "master" it. It all depends on your level of proficiency with your instrument.

In this case, your mind is the instrument, your memorization techniques are the music stand and the material you want to memorize is the music.

Is this rote learning? No.

The reason it isn't rote learning is because the only time you are going to look at the "sheet music" on your music stand is to "test" that you've gotten the memorized material right. When you haven't, you're going to refine the images and the action, and if necessary, work on the location of the memory as well. This is all part of mastering what you've memorized and developing perfect recall. It's also the reason I ask my readers and clients to use worksheets or Excel files to chart out their locations and the images and actions they used to memorize their target information.

This is also tied to the principle of location, believe it or not. Merely by having a "hard copy" somewhere, even if you don't look at it, the mind feels a sense of safety and security. We hate losing things, so when we allow ourselves to keep a record, even if we never actually refer to it other than for the purposes of testing once in awhile (once or twice a month is recommended for 2-3 months per word), we know it's there. It has a place and being able to conceive of that place in terms of a location has psychological benefits.

I use this musical metaphor because I play bass, and I can tell you that my fellow band members expect me to have the music down pat the first or second time I see it before we get into serious rehearsal and then performance without the safety net of sheet music. But it's still nice to have the sheet music back home. I don't know about you, but I'm not too proud to own a security blanket when it comes to something as precious as the material I've memorized.

1. Not Being Relaxed

Relaxation is a key component to memorization that no one I've read talks about. Maybe it's a just a given, but in my experience talking with readers and clients, there is so much stress around memorization and memory in general, that people often feel apprehensive when they sit down to work on their memories. So many of us love to claim that we have bad memories, and so when it comes time to memorize something, we're already in a defensive position.

This is not ideal. In fact, it just won't do.

As a reader of one of the Magnetic Memory series books, you know that I talk about the benefits of relaxation and give a few methods you can use before starting a memorization session. These include a particular kind of breathing and progressive muscle relaxation exercises.

Don't skip relaxation. Everything goes faster and smoother when you're relaxed. Your imagination, which naturally knows how to provide you with the perfect images, needs nothing more than a relaxed body to work with.

So the next time you want to memorize, remove all distractoins. Close the door, light a candel, meditate a little, do some pendulum breathing and do some progressive muscle relaxation. You'll be so glad you did.

That's all for this episode of Magnetic Memory Mondays. Feel free to share this entire article to your friends and social networks and let them know to email me at learnandmemorize@zoho.com to be included on the list.

And as always, teach someone what you've learned about memorization. It's the best way to deepen the techniques for yourself. And make the world a better place.

© 2013 Metivier Magnetic Memory Series.

All Rights Reserved. No part of this publication may be reproduced in any form or by any means, including scanning, photocopying, or otherwise without prior written permission of the copyright holder.

Disclaimer and Terms of Use: The Author and Publisher have strived to be as accurate and complete as possible in the creation of this book, notwithstanding the fact that he does not warrant or represent at any time that the contents within are accurate due to the rapidly changing nature of the Internet. While all attempts have been made to verify information provided in this publication, the Author and Publisher assumes no responsibility for errors, omissions, or contrary interpretation of the subject matter herein. Any perceived slights of specific persons, peoples, or organizations are unintentional.

This Edition, Copyright 2013